TEACHING AND LEARNING IN LATER LIFE

STUDIES IN EDUCATIONAL GERONTOLOGY

Series Editor

Frank Glendenning
Honorary Senior Research Fellow, Centre for Social Gerontology,
Keele University and Department of Continuing Education,
Lancaster University

This book is to be returned on
or before the date stamped below

Teaching and Learning in Later Life

Theoretical implications

FRANK GLENDENNING

with contributions from

SANDRA CUSACK
ROBERT ELMORE
CHRIS PHILLIPSON
ALEXANDRA WITHNALL

Aldershot • Burlington USA • Singapore • Sydney

Published by
Ashgate Publishing Ltd
Gower House
Croft Road
Aldershot
Hants GU11 3HR
England

Ashgate Publishing Company
131 Main Street
Burlington
Vermont 05401
USA

Ashgate website: http://www.ashgate.com

British Library Cataloguing in Publication Data
Teaching and learning in later life : theoretical
    implications. - (Studies in educational gerontology)
    1. Aged - Education 2. Aged - Education - Social aspects
    3. Learning, Psychology of, in old age
    I. Glendenning, Frank, 1921-
    374'.00846

Library of Congress Control Number: 00-132588

ISBN 1 84014 802 0

Printed and bound in Great Britain by MPG Books Ltd, Bodmin, Cornwall

Contents

v

Contributors

Sandra Cusack is Gutman-Gee Research Fellow in Educational Gerontology, Gerontology Research Centre and Lecturer in Third Age Learning, Faculty of Education, Simon Fraser University, Vancouver, Canada.

Robert Elmore is Emeritus Fellow of Kellogg College and formerly University Lecturer in Public Administration, University of Oxford, United Kingdom.

Frank Glendenning is Honorary Senior Research Fellow in Social Gerontology, Keele University and in Continuing Education, University of Lancaster, United Kingdom and a Joint Editor of *Education and Ageing*.

David James is Dean of Associated Institutions and formerly Professor of Educational Studies, University of Surrey, Guildford, United Kingdom. He was founder Chair of the Association for Education and Ageing.

Chris Phillipson is Professor and Director of the Centre for Social Gerontology, Keele University, United Kingdom.

Alexandra Withnall is non-clinical Lecturer in Gerontology, Postgraduate Medical School, Keele University, United Kingdom. She is current chair of the Association for Education and Ageing.

Foreword

This fascinating volume brings together the contributions of some of our most able and productive thinkers currently active in the field of teaching and learning in later life. They are drawn from fields as diverse as educational gerontology, social gerontology, public administration and continuing education. The juxtaposition of their contributions together with the skilful, integrative editing of Frank Glendenning has produced a feast of concepts and ideas from which all concerned with older learners must surely benefit.

Most of the contributors are active members of the Association for Education and Ageing and in that forum are no strangers to interdisciplinary debate. This is much in evidence in the way in which each author has drawn widely and freely on the thoughts of others. Such cross-fertilization helps in no small way in moving forward this emerging field of study, research and practice.

Although this book emphasizes particularly the moral, social, historical and educational perspectives of the key concepts running through it, those of us coming from other backgrounds (particularly the life sciences) will find our own ideas illuminated by and hopefully illuminating the questions which are raised.

Ageing, as the book's title suggests, is one such central theme. To the biologist, ageing refers to changes which occur to an organism as time passes. It is, therefore, a life-long process beginning at conception. It has dimensions both of growth and development and of decline and deterioration. When we are young growth dominates. As we get older the balance inevitably changes but at different rates, in different ways, in different individuals, in different circumstances. Such a dynamic view of a continuum for me is very helpful in exploring and making sense of the range of perspectives on the issues discussed. An explicit statement of the value of this approach comes on page 47 where Bernard and Phillips are quoted on their concept of 'an intergenerational life course perspective' which implies that we should focus on 'ageing' rather than 'old people' or 'old age'. Again Moody on page 14 is quoted as referring to 'the challenge of human development in the second half of life'. Phillipson in chapter 3 emphasizes the crucial role of the environment when he explores the concept of ageing as a socially constructed event, while Withnall in her excellent account of the life-course approach relates the ideas of learning choices to interaction between older people and the world around them.

Cusack in chapter 6 also has much to say about interaction with the environment while discussing empowerment. The ideas she develops relate to another concept of fundamental importance to the human biologist, namely environmental control. A major difference between human beings and other animals is the extent to which they control their environments or are controlled by their environments. As we reduce the opportunity for individuals to have control over their own lives for whatever reason, but here we are talking about ageing. Do we thereby begin to dehumanize them? Chapter 2 in talking about Freire's 'banking concept' of education illustrates this well by considering that often older learners are being 'domesticated' and, so 'inhibited' from realizing their full potential of 'being human'.

The second major theme of the book is of course 'learning and teaching' and again interdisciplinary considerations are extremely profitable. Learning is a fundamental biological and psychological process. All living creatures, in order to survive, must interact with their surroundings. Eating and breathing are essential for physical life. Taking in experiences and responding to them, activities in which learning is central, are essential for psychological well-being. Learning is the process by which we are sustained and developed through experience sand it occurs more or less continuously in ever part of our lives.

Each of the chapters in its own way examines the importance of a rich stimulating environment to promote mental health and the fact that we maintain our competence to benefit from such stimulation as we age. What is often lacking is the opportunity for many older people to be so sustained and stimulated, resulting in their demotivation, disempowerment and general disadvantage. Cusack in Chapter 6 and Glendenning in the final chapter are key contributions in this area.

Where does 'teaching' come into this debate? Chapters 7 and 8 are interesting treatments of this topic. Teaching involves creating opportunities for learning to occur. If you wish to master a particular skill, or body of knowledge, to change your attitudes or reappraise your ideas, you frequently need a specifically constructed learning environment to achieve your ends. Education is both the process and the product of such learning. Withnall (page 84) very helpfully discusses the place of education for older adults within the continuum of life-long learning. She and others implicitly reinforce the idea that creating your own learning opportunities are at least as important as those created for you by a teacher or adult educator. Perhaps this is a reflection of the point made by Glendenning that those who enjoyed successful education earlier in life are likely to do so again later on.

A final general point which this book brings home to me is the importance of 'motivation'. We all, whatever our ages, have a range of needs from those essential for basic biological survival to those concerning security, social acceptance, recognition and self-fulfilment. We try to produce behaviour to satisfy these needs. If we cannot then we are thwarted feeling insecure and threatened, rejected, devalued, unfulfilled. In a perfect world it would be possible for us each to satisfy our own needs without frustrating others. In reality, however, this is rarely the case particularly when more powerful people relate to less powerful. The teacher who satisfies his needs for security and status by denigrating and threatening his pupils, or the health care professional operating in a manner unconducive to the psychological comfort of the patient are examples of such social friction which have been partially overcome by making the less powerful person not so much a passive recipient but more an active participant in the relationship. Perhaps this same concept will be helpful in ameliorating some of the frustrations of older people when their needs are perceived inappropriately by others be they politicians, professionals or just people from other age groups. In most chapters one can pick out examples of older people being frustrated by others who through lack of knowledge and understanding, time or opportunity are putting their own needs first and ignoring the needs of those to whom they are relating. But putting this to rights however might well involve reconstructing human relationships in our society in general.

When existing bodies of knowledge which have developed separately are brought together, often substantial strides can be made in their areas of interaction. This I believe is the great strength of this volume. Its quality is a fitting tribute to its major contributor Frank Glendenning who remains for me the doyen of British writers in the field of education and ageing. He, together with his team of excellent colleagues have produced a scholarly and professional volume which will inform and inspire all who read it.

David James
University of Surrey

Introduction

While the title of this book of essays is *Teaching and Learning in later Life*, it is not a practical manual which is asking 'How?' It is rather an attempt to review the international phenomenon of the provision of self-help educational opportunities for those in later life, which is parallelled by the lack of mainstream educational provision and to ask the question 'Why?'

Throughout this project I have been supported and encouraged by my colleagues Sandra Cusack, Robert Elmore, Chris Phillipson and Alexandra Withnall. I want to thank them and most especially Robert Elmore himself who has been a pillar of strength from the outset through his continued advice and dependability, especially in pointing me to relevant source material which without his prompting, I would have otherwise missed. They have all given freely of their time and scholarship. But their welcome contributions to the discourse should not obscure the fact that I alone am responsible for any deficiencies in the remainder of the volume. The chapters by Sandra Cusack and Robert Elmore are both based on papers published originally in *Education and Ageing* 1999, Vol.15(1).

As usual Sue Allingham of the Keele University Centre for Social Gerontology has given unstintingly of her time and technical expertise in the type setting. I am also grateful to Anne Keirby, Claire Annals and Katherine Hodkinson, with her predecessors, at Ashgate Publishing for their patience and understanding in spite of numerous delays in completing the final manuscript.

I am also grateful to my wife Angela for her continual support and inspiration, when over the years my writing endeavours have provided a continuous invasion of domestic life.

It is now nearly 25 years since education for those in later life appeared on the adult education agenda as a matter for urgent attention and it is hoped that these papers may provide a useful basis at the turn of the century for future discussions concerning the concept of education for those in later life.

Frank Glendenning
Keele University

1 The education for older adults 'movement' : an overview

The provision of self-help education for older adults during the last quarter of a century began to develop in a very unplanned way while at the same time being widely regarded by those concerned as an integral part of the quality of life of older people, especially those in the Third Age.

The origin of the term 'third age' may be traced to the development of 'universités due troisième âge' (U3A) in the University of Toulouse, France in 1973 and which may now be found, loosely organised in many parts of the world. The purpose of the Toulouse scheme was to open up the university to retired people on a self-programming basis; to encourage mental and physical activity, thus to assist the healthy functioning of the faculties; to contribute to ageing research; and to encourage retired people to form themselves into active political groups (Reeves, 1980: p.19).

The concept of the third age, as Laslett has pointed out was a 'novelty' because it implied a different arrangement of stages in the life course from any that had previously been suggested, for example, Shakespeare's rendition of 'the seven ages of man' (Laslett, 1989: p.3). The First Age is childhood and adolescence; the Second Age is occupational and wage-earning activity; the Third Age is the period after the cessation of work; while the Fourth Age is when the very old are dependent on others and as Radcliffe has expressed it: 'A good third age can minimise the adjustments and deficits, and indeed the duration of the fourth age' (Radcliffe, 1984: p.62). The term 'third age', originally it was intended to embrace those over the age of 60/65, although increasingly in the 1990s it has come to be applied to those over 50, thus recognising the artificiality of the statutory retirement age in the face of increasing early retirement and redundancy from the workforce.

1

In the 1970s, even before the Toulouse and subsequent U3A experiments, a number of established groups of older people in different parts of Britain had begun to develop their own education and leisure activities and by 1980, the Forum for the Rights of Older People to Education (FREE) had been formed, led principally by some senior adult educators and staff of the ageing agencies. The purpose of FREE was to act as a focus for the collection and sharing of information about educational activities and opportunities for older people (Glendenning, 1985: p.109).

There were at least four reasons which led to this motivation towards education for older people. There has been an increase of popular awareness in the 1970s of the demographic factors which had contributed to an increasingly ageing population, with all the implications which that involved, and the potentially yawning vacuum of leisure time which the majority appeared to be facing.

Additionally, the 1950s and 1960s saw the beginnings of the pre-retirement education movement. This certainly led some educators to consider the role of education in helping older people to prepare for retirement from full-time paid work and in some ways it could be said to be a forerunner of the burst of interest in education for older adults in the 1970s and 1980s. But this development never became firmly embedded in the provision of further and higher education. The Pre-Retirement Association of Great Britain and Northern Ireland (PRA) had come into existence in 1964 (Phillipson, 1985: p.143).

The PRA was London-based with inadequate funding and by the mid-1970s questions were being raised about its raison d'être. The PRE movement as such had moved away from the London-based PRA and from its early educational roots and become merely a focus whereby local voluntary groups of PRA branches in different parts of the country provided local PRE courses which were primarily concerned with providing gobbets of information about, for example, health and ill-health in older age, advice about how to prepare financially for the period of life without paid work, leisure activities, relationships in later life etc. This activity exuded paternalism and what was absent was an interactive environment within which there could be an exchange of ideas in the groups about how to cope with the changed personal circumstances of retirement (a conclusion reached by two research studies which reported in the early 1980s - Coleman (1982); Phillipson and Strang (1983). A growing conviction about the importance of PRE finally led to the Department of Education and Science (DES) to recognise the PRA as the national focus for PRE, grant aiding its educational development work from 1982. A fuller account of these matters will be found in Glendenning, (1985).

The third reason for the development of the concept of the right of elderly people to education sprang from the education for older adults movement itself. Research-based writing on education and the older adult is virtually non-existent. The 'movement' evolved pragmatically as it became clear in the 1970s that the statutory provision of education for older people as part of the mainstream of the UK education system was becoming increasingly unlikely. Succeeding governments in the 1970s and 1980s made it clear that it was not on the national policy agenda, when education priorities were set, because of cost (Glendenning, 1976: p.62; 1985: p.112), although the DES in 1987 funded the Unit for the Development of Adult Continuing Education (UDACE) to carry out a mapping exercise on the provision of education for older people and to prepare a handbook of guidance for local educational authorities (This initiative did not progress immediately. But in 1987, the National Institute for Adult Continuing Education applied for funding to the National Lottery Charities Board and was able to set up three development teams as part of its *Older and Bolder Project,* to examine ways in which the wishes of older people with regard to educational activities could be identified and how a greater expansion for third age education might be achieved).

A further reason was the existence of the term 'lifelong education' itself. One of the earliest references to 'lifelong education' is to be found in a recommendation of UNESCO's International Committee for the Advancement of Adult Education in 1965:

> UNESCO should endorse the principle of 'lifelong education' ... which may be defined briefly as 'the animating principle of the whole process of education, regarded as continuing throughout an individual's life from his earliest childhood to the end of his days and therefore calling for integrated organisation ... to be achieved vertically through the duration of life and horizontally to cover all the various aspects of the life of individuals and societies (cited in Jessup, 1969: p.vii).

More precisely, the General Conference of UNESCO in 1976 made specific recommendations about educational activities for older people which should be designed:

(a)   to give all a better understanding of contemporary problems and of the younger generation;

(b)   to help acquire leisure skills, promote health and find increased meaning in life;

(c)   to provide a grounding in the problems facing retired people and in ways of dealing with such problems for the benefit of those who are on the point of leaving working life;

(d)   to enable those who have left working life to retain their physical and intellectual faculties and to continue to participate in community life and also to give them access to fields of knowledge or types of activity which have not been open to them during their working life (UNESCO, n.d. 1979?: p.11).

3

This was a remarkably advanced statement for 1976 embodying the term coined by UNESCO, *éducation permanente*. From the mid-1980s onwards, such a formulation increasingly resembled themes and topics which came to characterise the transactions of many organisations working with older people, but in the UK, such transactions were carried on outside the statutory sector by a variety of self-help groups. Furthermore, the meaning of 'lifelong education' and 'lifelong learning' in the UK has been continually demeaned by utterances of the Department of Education and Science (DES) and its successor the Department for Education and Employment (DfEE), which as recently as 1995 published a consultation document, *Lifetime Learning*. This was concerned with urging employers to take training seriously as an implication of vocational lifetime learning, stressing 'the importance of a highly motivated, flexible and well-qualified workforce to the United Kingdom's international competitiveness' (DfEE, 1995: p.7), thus stifling any informed debate about the understanding of instrumental and expressive education in relation to education for older adults. It is perhaps a sign of the times in Europe as a whole that when the European Union designated 1996 as 'The European Year of Lifelong Learning, Education and Training', it described lifelong learning as 'a key factor in the personal development of individuals and for a European model of competitiveness and growth'. Although EurolinkAge noted with approval that 'In spite of a clear emphasis on youth and vocational training, older people are specifically mentioned as a target group' (*EurolinkAge Bulletin*, 1995: p.10).

Thus in spite of this latter confusion, and in spite of the UK's inability in social policy terms to recognise the legitimacy of older adults' learning, the last twenty-five years have seen a burgeoning of self-initiated activity mainly by older people themselves.

The development of the University of the Third Age in the UK has developed in an entirely different way from the U3A of the Francophone countries. We saw earlier (p.1) that the first U3A in Toulouse was based on a desire to involve retired people in intellectual and physical pursuits and to enable them to develop their political awareness in a university setting. British Universities had been involved in adult education for over a century through the medium of university extra-mural and adult education courses. The French had not been involved in adult education to any great extent at all. However, as a result of educational changes in the 1960s, legislation in 1968 declared that universities must be open to all, committed to lifelong education and to organising educational activities with all interested parties. Legislation in 1971 also decreed that all firms with more than ten employees should pay one per cent of their salaries bill towards the lifelong learning programme in the university, industrial and voluntary sectors.

It was within this atmosphere that the first U3A was formed in Toulouse in 1973, when one hundred third age students attended specially designed university courses during the examination and vacation period. Success was so swift that other groups were formed very quickly in other parts of France. By 1984, it was estimated that 100,000 people were enrolled in U3A activities (Brasseul, 1984). No single U3A developed in exactly the same way as the one in Toulouse. But the purpose of involving retired people in university studies has remained the same. By 1995, there were 1700 university of the third age-type organisations world-wide, including the Francophone countries, Australia, China, Finland, Italy, Poland, Slovenia and the UK.

The U3A in the UK was formed in 1981 (Glendenning, 1985: p.122). It did not however develop into a campus-based organisation as in France. Rather, noting that 'university' is not a popular concept, the British reverted to the medieval idea of the university as a community of scholars 'joined together in the selfless pursuit of knowledge and truth for its own sake' (Midwinter, 1984: p.4). This was a cosmetic device. Midwinter described the use of the title 'U3A' as a unshamed burglary of the continental usage and regarded the British U3A as 'cocking a perky snook at the conventional university' (Midwinter, 1984: pp.3-4). In this, he was in agreement with the founders of the French U3A. 'Education for older adults represents a real challenge to the traditional model of education geared towards production, profitability and social advancement' (Brasseul, 1985). And as Midwinter warmed to his theme, he saw U3As as slowly demonstrating that ordinary folk with reasonable aid and development were altogether capable of inventing their own educational destiny in their own back parlour (Midwinter, 1984: p.14). He believed that they provided, in the main for those who cannot or do not wish to travel far, who wish to join together, without the stress of academic rivalry, with usually, small numbers of their fellows in often times uninhibiting and unostentatious places (Midwinter, 1984: p.14).

The educational system had brought this revolt upon itself. It had developed a type of elitism (especially in the university adult education departments) through which it wished to create its own programme of educational and social events, in its own way, at a venue and time of its own choosing. It had come to depend also on a pedagogic (teacher/taught) relationship which included a guaranteed attendance and compulsory written work which in the 1970s and 1980s was increasingly resented by some older adult students (Glendenning, 1997: p.126), thus ignoring the advice of those who had been urging for some time that the task of education for older adults was to arouse social awareness, rather than to provide content, to enhance the consciousness of the elderly in relation to themselves and their social setting (Groombridge, 1982: p.318). Furthermore, 'the organisation of the learning experience must allow the individual to regain control over what is produced and created' (Allman, 1984: p.87). Gibson was to emphasise this later (1986: p.6), saying that 'emancipation is a key word in education, because it implies gaining the power to control one's own life'.

It would be a mistake to think that this 'revolt' was confined to U3A. Peter Laslett and Eric Midwinter were the great UK polemicists for third age education in the 1980s and while Laslett promulgated his National Educational Charter in 1980, claiming that:

> The British, over 60, are the worst instructed people, not only in our own population, but also among the advanced western countries as a whole. They are the least educated community of native English speakers (Laslett, 1984: p.20).

He based this judgement on the fact that the number of years of compulsory schooling in Britain in the 1920s was less than in North America and Australia or New Zealand, and Midwinter had already expressed a similar view:

> It is a harsh irony that the [present] British elderly left school with precious little to show for it; they were the tax and rate payers who, during their working lives, subsidised the most gigantic educational bonanza in our history; that is, after 1945 and especially in the 1960s; and who on retirement, have little or no call upon the education service (Midwinter, 1982: p.7).

In the same book Midwinter showed that, largely as a result FREE (see p.2 above), it had become possible to find out and describe that had already begun to be acknowledged as widespread developments of work among older people which were in the self-help mode and in the main quite outside mainstream educational provision (pp.32-40). Groombridge also returned to similar developments, a few years later (Groombridge, 1989: pp.193-6) drawing attention to the way in which to improve the quality of educational activities and opportunities in later life, he instanced the need for formal, informal and non-formal agencies to distance themselves from simplistic views about older people's educational interests and capabilities, in order to find new ways of collaboration and curriculum development, because the take-up of educational opportunities by older people was very low.

For a long time, it was believed that two per cent of the over-60s participated in educational activities in the USA (Harris, 1974). In the UK, in 1982, the Centre for Policy on Ageing inserted a question in the Quota Omnibus survey of the national Opinion Polls Market Research Ltd. The question was: "Are you at present undertaking a part-time educational course?" Of those over 60 years of age, only two per cent were engaged in any form of education from social class E, whereas eight or nine per cent of those from class A and B claimed some form of educational participation (Midwinter, 1982: p.20) Abrams in an attempt to explain this disappointing phenomenon referred to the unfavourable image of education (teaching by rote and use of the cane during school days) and the unattractive provision of educational courses by institutions and organisations specialising in adult education (Abrams, 1981: pp.2-3).

In 1990, Percy reviewed the National Institute of Adult Education's survey in 1967-8; three data sets: the General Household Surveys of 1977, 1981 and 1983; and a survey carried out by the Advisory Council of Adult Continuing Education (ACACE) in 1980 and he reported:

These surveys just about enable us to ascribe to a generalised statement such as this: "We know that for those of pensionable age (and thereabouts) current (i.e. at the time of asking) participation in classes (i.e. all classes; work-related education may make little difference to the figures) is in the range of two to seven per cent. About two-thirds of this age-group have never participated in classes (Percy, 1990: p.31).

In 1997, the National Institute of Adult Continuing Education (NIACE) carried out a survey based on a sample of 4,000 people over 17. This showed that nine per cent of the 55-64 age group and nine per cent of those over 65 were either studying at the time of the survey or had studied within the last three years (Sargant, 1997). This is an indication that there was an increase in organised educational activities over the previous decade (Schuller and Bostyn, 1992: p.11). The latter were commissioned by the Carnegie UK Trust to participate in the largest investigation into matters concerning the third age in Britain the Third Age between 1991 and 1992, with responsibility for the Learning and Education Study. In their report they found that roughly two-thirds of those between 50 and state retirement age left school at 15 or earlier, compared to about one third of those who are younger. Sixty per cent of those between 50 and 69 have never obtained any formal qualifications and have had very few opportunities for continuing education compared to only 18 per cent of those in their 20s. 'Each successive generation has had more access to education but the older generations have not caught up' (Schuller and Bostyn, 1992: p.87), thus confirming the claims of Laslett and Midwinter, ten years before. Schuller and Bostyn concluded that about three-quarter of a million 'third agers' enrol annually in some kind of formal adult education and a similar number receive some form of organised training, which suggests that roughly one in ten of the over-50s (Carnegie's definition of the 'third age') take part each year in formal learning. In addition, at least 1.5 million older adults, and probably many more engage in informal learning activities (Schuller and Bostyn, 1992: p.39). The National Adult Learning Survey (NALS), reporting in 1998, went further, saying that of the sample studied, 64 per cent had left school by the age of 16 (see further, next chapter).

It has been argued in the past that an emphasis on the need for education for older people is ageist, ghettoising older people as 'the geological model of education, whereby people move through life trapped in a peer group layer' (Hunter, 1982: pp.1 and 22). Adult education, it has been claimed, should be inclusive of all age groups and not single out older people. But that is to deny the true meaning of lifelong education. Midwinter has said: 'Education needs to be lifelong because life is long and the issues which challenge us continue to change in sometimes bewildering patterns from cradle to grave' (Midwinter, 1982: p.7). And as long ago as 1978, Tyler took down and throughly dusted the issue of separate or integrated provision:

> The two major assumptions that must be challenged are, firstly, that all people over a given arbitrary age (60 or 65 for instance) can be lumped together and dealt with as though they were a homogeneous group; secondly, the assumption that the elderly, as a group are in some specific way disadvantaged educationally because of the one factor of their age. If these two assumptions are challenged then the question as to whether provision for elderly people should or should not be separated from the provision for the general population becomes easier to resolve. This is because the elderly can be separated into different target groups, in exactly the same way as with the adult population at large (Tyler, 1979: p.10).

But Tyler added realistically that because of the context of existing provision:

> Older people are more likely to enrol for classes held in the daytime, near to their homes, on a convenient bus route, and in better months of the year. In other words, an age-segregated class may happen, almost without thought on the part of the tutor or the organiser, as a consequence of other decisions (Tyler, 1979: p.11).

But this process had already begun in the 1970s, by older students making their own arrangements and voting with their feet! The 1980s, as we have seen, saw this process develop even further. It is instructive therefore to ask at this stage, given that all these practical developments had taken place in the 1970s and 1980s, what was believed to be the purpose of third age education?

Loring for example in 1978 suggested that 'by the regrooming of both mental and physical capacities, rehabilitation of the life force occurs for more satisfying later years' (Loring, 1978: p.viii), thus foreshadowing Radcliffe's comments on the fourth age, already mentioned (p.2 above). Agruso, also in 1978, saw education as the means of 'surviving in an enormously complex environment by continuing to learn new things' (Agruso, 1978: p.vii). In the 1980s, Midwinter suggested that:

> Ultimately the object is that the life of each individual person might be enhanced by educational provision in its broadest sense ... It is difficult to isolate 'the elderly' from the rest of the population and 'education' from what is termed a full and active life ... [the] needs of retired people ... must not be

considered apart from those other sections of the populace with similar requirements ... [and] educational facilities are just part of a wide range of constructive activities ... for a well rounded retirement (Midwinter, 1982: p.1).

Groombridge however has asserted that 'what emerges from the available evidence is that the crucial stimulus to participation is the sense of personal efficiency and competence which in turn is strongly related to social status' (Groombridge, 1989: p.187).

The single most influential figure in the USA in this field of study has been D.A. Peterson and in the UK we have been greatly influenced by his definitions of 'educational gerontology' (Peterson, 1976, 1978, 1980, 1983). (See also Glendenning 1985, 1987, 1990, 1997).

In his book *Facilitating Education for Older Learners*, published in 1983, he wrote:

Education may be designed to help the older person to understand the changes occurring within society, to be able to anticipate changes, and to prepare for them. Likewise, education may help to clarify the physical and psychological changes occurring within the individual that may cause concern if they are not differentiated from pathological conditions that occasionally occur in later life (Peterson, 1983: p.9).

As a result of the Royal Society of Arts' study of *Education for Capability*, Walker commented that 'the current hegemony of instrumental and content-based education-as-training will remain unshaken for some time to come, but unless alternatives are developed there will be nothing to meet the demand for so-called non-vocational education' (Walker, 1985: p.201).

Nothing has changed since then and this is precisely what has added momentum to the self-help mode of development as increasing numbers of older students turned their backs on the need for capability and competencies preferring rather to 'pursue education for its own sake'. Lowy, in his text *Why Education in the Later Years?* (1986) argues pragmatically that educating older people can improve their well-being and further the welfare of society as a whole, quoting extensively from the recommendations of the 1981 White House Conference on Aging and the 1983 United Nations World Assembly on Aging.

By 1990, Peterson was reflecting confidently that in the USA:

Educational programs for older people have now developed to such a point that we can begin to gain some perspective on their growth and to identify some of the trends that have emerged, four of which I discuss. First, there now seems to be general acceptance that we are living in a learning society, in which people of every age will be required to expand their knowledge and skills in order to survive and prosper and the second implication is that the rationale for older people has modified the orientation of many instructional programs. Third, education for older people is no longer a modest undertaking rating little time or interest and relegated to the smallest division of an institution ... Fourth, as the enrolment of older people increases, institutions that in the past have simply encouraged older people to participate in their regular programs are beginning to develop special offerings exclusively for them (Peterson, 1990: pp.15-16).

Peterson went on to describe what the implication of this situation is: (1) how to deal with the stereotyping of the elderly? (b) How is this work to be financed and resourced? Federal and foundation funds are inadequate. (c) The need to improve the quality and efficiency of instruction. (d) Expand the use of the media for educating older people. (e) The need for the inclusion of older participants from all socio-economic levels.

What this reveals is that a decade ago in the USA there was the same anticipation as in the UK that the 'education for older adults movement' had arrived and was there for all to see. In effect, this was an over-simplification in both countries, because although both countries can demonstrate considerable elements of success (Peterson, for example, demonstrating that some American institutions had begun to accommodate the educational needs of older adults (Peterson, 1983: p.240), in neither country (or elsewhere for that matter), except perhaps China (Du Zicai, 1994, 1998) can it be demonstrated that education for older adults is on the national educational or social policy agenda. It still has not achieved the status of legitimation. It is our conviction that because of the nature of the development, at no stage have serious questions been asked about this development. Moody has suggested that 'public policy still looks on the education of old people as being merely a frill and not as having anything to do with human development in the second part of life' (Moody, 1988: p.212). It is these matters that we will seek to address at a later stage.

Historically, when in the early 1970s, adult educators in the USA began to reflect on the significance of third age education (they did not use this term then) for education as a whole, it was recognised that so far education for older adults had developed in an *ad hoc* way and little thought had been given to the relation of the phenomenon to the growing body of multi-disciplinary knowledge in the field of gerontology. In 1970, Howard McClusky, who was Professor of Education at the University of Michigan with a strong personal link with the University's Institute of Gerontology, developed a Doctoral programme in his Department with the title 'Educational Gerontology'. From this idea was born a number of actions which resulted in a national conference on educational gerontology at Virginia Beach, Virginia in 1976, which in turn led to the founding of the journal *Educational Gerontology* together with the publication of the conference papers *Introduction to Educational Gerontology* (Sherron and Lumsden, 1978), which had gone into several editions by the 1990s.

When in the UK, in the late 1970s, we began to become familiar with these papers and the journal, it became apparent to us that the practical and methodological side of education for older adults was not developing and that the term 'educational gerontology' was being used in America in an inclusive way to cover aspects of behavioural psychology in later life and gerontology teaching as well. This found no resonance in the UK situation where social gerontology did not become established as an academic subject until the late 1980s.

In an attempt to emphasise the importance of educational gerontology as a new field of study, in the UK, *Educational Gerontology: International Perspectives* was published in 1985. This introduced a clear distinction between 'educational gerontology' which had everything to do with the teaching of older adults, including tutor training, syllabus construction, organisation and management and public education about an ageing society, and 'gerontological education' which was concerned with the teaching of gerontology to professionals, para-professionals and volunteers (Glendenning, 1985: pp.31-53; 1987, 1990). For some, this seemed to be an arcane discussion. But it was argued, unless we can clarify these two elements, it will not be possible to develop a theoretical base for the work.

Adult educators and those concerned with the eduction for older adults movement formed themselves into the *Association for Educational Gerontology* in 1985. The Association published its own refereed journal, the *Journal for Educational Gerontology* from 1986. It soon became clear that this was a difficult undertaking because of the scarcity of suitable material for publication and there was additionally a complete absence of practice-centred material. As a result 'educational gerontology' was used as an inclusive term as far as the content of the journal was concerned and for a variety of reasons the title of the journal was changed in 1994 to *Education and Ageing*, while the Association changed its name in 1998 to *The Association for Education and Ageing* believing that this title better described the way in which it had developed. The stated commitment in the Association's constitution is to education for older adults, public education about ageing and the training of gerontology professionals, para-professionals and volunteers.

Throughout the 1990s, there was a regular exchange of views in both the journal and at professional conferences about the meaning of educational 'gerontology', the scope of this debate will be discussed in the next two chapters and the remainder of the book will attempt to carry the debate forward.

2 Some critical implications

2 Some critical implications

Introduction

We have already noted, although deliberately not going into any great detail, that one of the international social phenomena of our time has been the expansion, during the last twenty-five years of the 'education for older adults movement'. This has been well documented elsewhere (and see Glendenning, 1983, 1985, 1997, 1998).

It began, as we have seen, for a number of reasons. There was the growing awareness demographically of the vastly increased numbers of people over 50 or 60, who were about to face one-third of their life in 'retirement', having ceased their full-time paid work. Observers were concerned about how they were to fill in their time. Second, there was the revolt against statutory educational provision, which was failing to meet the needs of older people, partly because of the unsuitability of programmes, partly because of the ambience of the venue, and partly because of transport and finance.

This turning away from traditional adult education led to the development of self-help education, which in the UK proved to be more successful in small towns and rural areas than in larger conglomerations (Midwinter, 1984: p.13; 1996: p.32; Glendenning, 1998: p.127). Third, numbers of adult educators, with a sense and appreciation of the past, recognised that the majority of those over 60 in the UK had been early school leavers with all that that implied. The most recent reliable statistic is to be found in the National Adult Learning Survey 1997 (NALS) which took its sample from those between 16 and 69. In spite of the age range, the Survey demonstrated, as we have seen, that 64 per cent of the whole sample had left school by the age of 16 (NALS, 1998: p.14). Fifty per cent of the respondents said that nothing would encourage them to do some learning if a suitable course was available; another seven per cent thought that they might engage in some learning if money worries were removed and six per cent, if it would lead to a better job. When asked about the perceived benefits of learning, 64 per cent mentioned improved knowledge, 61 per cent found learning interesting, 59 per cent learnt new skills and 55 per cent spoke of enjoyment (NALS, 1998: pp.226-39). In the nature of the case, this was self-reported information and must be regarded as anecdotal. It has seemed over the years that the repeated dependence on self-evaluation and anecdotal evidence has militated against a watertight case being marshalled to achieve public legitimation and financial support for third age education within the sphere of mainstream educational provision.

Questions

Indeed, no questions were every asked like why do we teach the elders? Whose interests are really being served? Who controls the learning process? Why is education 'good for people'? and how is quality of life enhanced by education? Gibson, for example, was critical of what theorists called 'instrumental rationality', regarding it as being preoccupied with means rather than ends, with method and efficiency rather than purposes. 'It limits itself to 'How to do it?' questions rather than 'Why do it?' or 'Where are we going?' questions. (This reveals) the desire to control and to dominate, to exercise surveillance and power over others' (Gibson, 1986: p.7).

Lifelong learning

In this volume we are asserting that education in an ageing society can no longer be tied exclusively to younger people. Even the government mantra of 'lifelong learning' admits that education and training is necessary for some as they grow older, so that knowledge may be renewed and skills updated. It is just as true for people who have passed mid-life and, who may require retraining after they have been made redundant in their full-time job. Harrison has claimed that 'we require a rationale (for third age education) which is more in tune with political and economic reality (Harrison, 1988: p.14) and the American gerontologist. H.R. Moody, went further, (in a passage already noted in the previous chapter), suggesting that 'we need to ask basic questions about what it means for older people to learn and develop in the last stage of life ... Public policy still looks on the education of old people as a frill, strictly as a matter of private decision, and above all, something that does not cost money and certainly is not worth spending money on ... [It is not simply] a way of filling in time for old folks. It is nothing less than the challenge of human development on the second half of life ' (Moody, 1988: p.212).

It has been borne in on us more and more in recent years that in today's political climate, beginning in the UK with the policies of the New Right in the 1980s, that 'education for older adults' only has slogan status and what is important is that we should cease to domesticate and marginalise older people and enable them to become empowered so that they can take control of decisive elements of their own lives. Rather than paying lip service to the normal rationale that education is 'good' for older adults and can enhance their quality of life, we need to seek a new paradigm for education for older persons.

Critical theory

Just as critical gerontology in recent years has become an essential tool in the training of gerontology professionals, enabling them to become critical and reflective in the ways in which they respond to social policy and practice, so we we need to apply critical theory to educational gerontology itself (see Phillipson in the following chapter). Concepts and theories are the best tools we have for understanding social phenomena. Concepts and theories, rather than anecdotal evidence should provide the framework for our search for the legitimation of educational gerontology as a field of study. Taken overall, the fact that third age education only has slogan status after 25 years of debate 'highlights a massive exclusion of older people from learning opportunities which might add substantially to the quality of 20 or more years spent in retirement ... It would be no exaggeration to argue that without effective educational provision the years in retirement are wasted ' (Phillipson, 1998: p.133).

Critical theory in the tradition of the Frankfurt school is concerned (1) to interpret the meaning of human existence, (2) to examine the problems of social justice, and (3) how to understand the cultural tendencies of everyday life (Gibson, 1986: pp.20 ff; Morrow, 1991: pp.28 ff.).

One of the consequences of applying critical theory to educational gerontology is that it leads us to recognise the need for a paradigm shift. A paradigm is a tool of analysis, making sense of complex phenomena. Third age educators need to move away from their implicitly functionalist approach, where older people are seen as a social problem and a disadvantaged group, to a socio-economic framework which examines society's treatment of older people. Educational provision for older adults tends to be shackled to the functionalist paradigm and linked with notions that education can have an ameliorating effect on the anticipated difficulties and problems of older people by improving their quality of life, (a view made popular in the third age movement during the last 20 years). There is for example the anecdotally-based belief that education can be the means of avoiding institutionalisation in old age, therefore saving the expenditure of public money. No scientific research in the UK has ever validated this claim

15

(Numbers of published papers in the USA have broached this claim. But no unified text has ever brought together this research).

Such liberal ideology is the same ideology which believes that education is not only a good thing in itself, but works positively towards eradicating the inequalities and injustices that are evident in our experience day by day. Gibson for example recognised that such opinions had been hypothesised in educational assumptions for a century, but that this was manifestly not the case and 'education has neither succeeded well for all classes, nor has it removed underlying inequalities and injustices' (Gibson, 1986: p.46).

By extension, the inherent promises that liberal ideology makes for education in later life are without foundation and will never eradicate the socially created injustices which are the experience of so many older people.

The functionalist paradigm

At the core of the functionalist paradigm is the notion that:

> ... old age is essentially viewed as a problem of adult socialisation: how could older people be reintegrated within a social order which was undergoing social change? (Fennell et al., 1989: p.43).

This functionalist perspective, as Fennell et al. point out, had two main variants: (1) role and activity theory and (2) the disengagement hypothesis. In respect of the former, functionalism gave particular emphasis to the impact of social roles and in this context, the loss of work role was seen by Talcott Parsons nearly 60 years ago, as creating for men a major crisis of identity:

> Retirement leaves the older man in a peculiarly functionless situation, cut off from the most important interests and activities of the society (Parsons, 1942: p.616).

As the years passed, such a view became modified, not least because of the effect of women's studies and the subsequent development of gender awareness. The disengagement theory also became very influential in the 1960s as we will see in chapter five. But 'a common criticism of functionalist theories is that they simply provide a convenient rationalisation of power relationships' (Fennell et al., 1989: p.47), and it must be said that Parson's views of old age led to the ameliorating effects of education, especially for older adults. However, gerontologists became increasingly concerned with the meaning of old age itself (Phillipson, 1998) and greater emphasis was placed on the need to establish a role for older people in society and on the finding out of what older people themselves wished to do or to

16

be. When they retired from full-time paid work and if and when they realised that disengagement is not a universal experience spread over many years, it became recognised that there was a heuristic value in the way in which the functional paradigm led to a discussion of these issues when critical theory was applied.

The context of old age

During the late 1960s and 1970s, there was a growing interest in the actual context of old age. While the functionalist paradigm emphasised stability and adjustment in later life, the social constructivist perspective led to a clearer perception of some of the experiences of those growing old and the popularisation of the term, 'the social construction of ageing' through the defining work of Townsend (1991), Phillipson (1982) and Walker (1981, 1986). Fennell et al. described it:

> Old age can be viewed as a social construction formed out of demographic, economic and work processes. However, old age has been given a distinctive shape by the ideas and beliefs of, first, older people themselves (and those about to reach old age), and secondly by those who work on their behalf - doctors, social workers, health visitors, district nurses and many others (Fennell et al., 1989: p.39).

Implicit in this definition is the view that ageing is a social rather than a biological construction, because as Estes and Binney (1989) showed, the biomedicalisation of gerontology had led to what became known as the 'disease model of old age'.

Townsend for example sees dependency in old age as being structured by economic and political forces:

> In the everyday management of the economy and the administration and development of social institutions the position of the elderly is subtly shaped and changed. The policies which determine the conditions and welfare of the elderly are not just the reactive policies represented by the statutory social services, but the much more generalised and institutionalised policies of the state which maintain and change the social structure (Townsend, 1986: p.21).

The functionalist, social constructivist and biomedical paradigms have then provided an incomplete understanding of how the advanced capitalist economies impact on older people and create difficulties in their lifestyles and culture, especially in retirement. Estes has suggested that this requires an analysis of how age divisions are created in society. This 'begins with the proposition that the status and resources of the elderly, and even the experience of old age itself, are

17

conditioned by one's location in the social structure ... [and] the factors that shape that location' (Estes, 1986: p.121).

One conclusion to be drawn from this is that an exploration of the relationship between capitalist society and ageing needs to occupy a more central position in educational and social gerontology as Phillipson's examination of this (1982, 1998) has shown.

Additionally, education for older adults should be a means of raising the consciousness of older people, about their role in society (what Paulo Freire (1972) called 'conscientisation') as well as being about their quality of life and their personal growth and self-fulfilment. At the moment, third age education merely leads to the domestication of older people. That is to say that by asking no questions about the location of older people in the social structure, it encourages them to accept and conform to society as they have perceived it.

Liberation and empowerment

Allman has demonstrated how Freire in his *Pedagogy of the Oppressed* 'depicts a process of education and learning which is one of liberation through a denunciation of structures that are dehumanising' (Allman, 1984: p.82). Through working with Mexican peasants, he believed that the traditional forms of education were oppressive and relied on what he called 'the banking concept', whereby knowledge is simply deposited in the minds of learners in order that they can be socialised into their culture or society. Learners are thus domesticated and are inhibited from realising their full potential of 'being human'. If on the other hand, learners are given the opportunity to exercise full control of their own thinking and learning, significant transformations can take place in both the individual and within society. Allman's view is that Freire's ideas help us to see how we might create these transformations for older people through a more liberating and empowering form of education than is currently available.

Hegemony

Friere's concept is similar to Antonio Gramsci's (1971) notion of 'hegemony', a term that Gramsci used to refer to the process of achieving dominance without opposition, although he cautioned that hegemony should not be seen as a mechanistic procedure, but rather as a dynamic and creative process, which occurs with the consent of those involved. Hence our earlier questions, "Whose interests are really being served?" and "Who controls the learning process?" and the emphasis that our life experiences continues to be a learning process and that reflection on these experiences can be liberating.

Allman refers to 'hegemony' as 'common sense' or 'the vast range of notions that have to do with preserving and guaranteeing the position in society of those who hold the real power' (Allman, 1984: p.83). She went on to reflect that 'hegemony is not opposed by those who derive no benefit from it, because even the oppressed accept hegemonic notions as reality or common sense'. In emerging nations, or those in a state of upheaval, hegemony is maintained through the military apparatus of the state. Therefore it is more visible or less subtle than it is in mature nation-states, where it is maintained through the apparatus of civil society, such as the media and education'. The practice of pedagogy with adult learners is one example of the subtle influence of 'hegemony' in our society. The process of adults coming to control their own thinking and learning can only take place through the creation of alternative structures and conditions for learning. This will depend largely on changing the relationship of learners and teachers with knowledge (Allman, 1984: p.84).

The need for a theoretical framework

Londoner is one of the few commentators who has expressed the need for the development of a theoretical framework for examining the educational wants of older people (Londoner, 1990: p.85). But there is a distinction between needs and wants. Needs tend to be identified by the professional educator through an analysis of the older person's circumstances, whereas wants tend to be the strong desires and preferences which are expressed by older people. Havighurst in the mid-1960s developed the terms *expressive* and *instrumental* education. By 'expressive education' he meant education for a goal that lies within the act of learning, or is so closely related to it that the act of learning appears to be the goal. He saw this kind of education as 'a kind of consumption of time and energy for present gain', i.e. participating in learning activity which yielded immediate satisfaction simply because of taking part (what we sometimes call 'education as self-fulfilment'). 'Instrumental education' for Havighurst meant education for a goal that is delayed and lies outside the act of education. Education is the means of changing the learner's situation, with an expectation of future gain at the conclusion of the activity (Havighurst, 1964: pp.17-38). In Britain this polarisation became a battle-ground from the 1970s onwards in adult education policy and practice as between non-vocational and vocational education, vocational education being greatly favoured in official educational policy because of its significance for skills and ability and its potential for the development of the market economy.

Londoner, based on American experience, dismissed this distinction on the grounds that what we should be doing was to analyse how older learners optimised what Talcott Parsons called 'their goal gratifications' (Parsons, 1942:

p.48). Londoner really sees the distinction as being between immediate and long-term goals (1980: p.86). What is the goal of the older learner in deciding to follow a particular course of learning? Is it for self-fulfilment and a sense of pleasure and well-being in the present, or is there a long-term aim to develop new skills either for meeting the demands of the later years or contributing to wealth creation? Such questions are not usually heard in discussion about education and older adults, nor are questions about knowledge and power.

The moral element

Very many older people see their lives as apparently out of control because they are determined by factors which inhibit and prevent them from gaining power over their lives. There is therefore a moral element to education and there must be a commitment to transform the conditions which promote the disempowerment of older people. Most of the evidence about those who already participate in third age learning activities is that they received education beyond secondary schooling, are middle-class and economically secure (Schuller and Bostyn, 1992: p.14; NALS, 1998: pp.32 ff.). As a result, it is always necessary to challenge the relationship between teacher and taught. Many questions about the learning relationship are being ignored. Teachers and facilitators need to ask 'Where do the ideas that I embody in my work come from historically? and why did I adopt them and why do I continue to endorse them?' 'Whose interests do these ideas serve?' 'What are the power relationships involved in my work with older people?'

Andragogy

When teachers and/or facilitators follow a conventional pedagogic approach they are unconsciously controlling the learning process and determining what the learners should know or discover. This approach has been described by Knowles as 'teacher-directed education' (Knowles, 1988). Knowles, as is well-known, favoured the andragogical model of education which implied the need of the learner to know, the learner's self-concept, the learner's experience, a readiness to learn, and motivation. In this context, both teachers and learners have the potential for future development and in their peer learning group to share the decision-making process with regard to content and method of learning. Here, negotiation, and continuous evaluation and reflection, in relation to learning or thinking and in relation to the process that is unfolding in the group are essential, but difficult without imagination and training.

20

This is a far cry from the instrumental rationality that is so much a part of conventional educational provision for older adults and which we discussed at the beginning of this chapter. It results in the exercise of hegemony, hierarchy, domination and power in the education of older people and does not admit that the implication of the individual learner gaining power over elements of his/her thinking and of his/her life precludes any notion of how to enhance individual autonomy and creativity which may be seen as the primary concern of the education of older people. Furthermore, the importance of life experience and reflecting on it as part of the learning process is both liberating and empowering.

Critical theory and education

This, as Gibson pointed out, marks out the true distinctiveness of the application of critical theory to education. 'Not only does it provide enlightenment (deeper understanding of our true interests); rather more than that (indeed because of that), it can set us free. Unlike scientific theory, it claims to provide guidance as to what to do'. He continues: 'There are clearly immense problems attaching to a theory which not only argues that it can reveal the world more clearly, but also asserts that it can be used to change the world, to liberate from inequalities and unfair restrictions' (Gibson, 1986: p.6). Later in his book Gibson expands on this and argues that such liberal ideology is the same century-old ideology which believed that education is not only a good thing in itself but works positively towards eradicating the inequalities and injustices that are evident in our experience day by day. Manifestly he says, such promises have not been redeemed (Gibson, 1986: p.46). By extension, the inherent promises that liberal ideology continues to make for education in later life, are without foundation and will never eradicate the socially created injustices which are the experience of so many older people.

The intellectual basis of education for older adults and educational gerontology is seriously under threat. Its theory is both disputed and discounted. If critical theory teaches us anything, it is that there is an indissolubility between theory and practice. Theory can be derived from the actual problems, concepts and language of practitioners themselves. During the last quarter of a century during the growth of the 'education for older adults' movement', in the anti-intellectual atmosphere of British life, it is notable that practitioners have been silent about their practice both orally and in print. The special commitment of critical theory is to emancipation. This in itself can help to reveal distortions in practice which frequently prevent rational discourse about the theory which justifies the practice.

What is required, as has been indicated above, is a shift away from the functionalist paradigm, where older people are viewed as a social problem and a disadvantaged group, to a socio-political framework which examines society's treatment of older people as Estes and others have suggested. Groombridge, writing in the early 1980s, echoed this:

> The first task of education is to arouse self-awareness rather then to provide content, to enhance the consciousness of the elderly in relation to themselves and to their social setting, to strengthen their self-esteem and to encourage their questioning of hidden aspirations (Groombridge, 1982: p.315).

In their excellent *Learning to Grow Older and Bolder,* Carlton and Soulsby wrote:

> There continues to be a compounding *class* divide affecting chances to return to learn. Older people who have experienced post-school education and training, and those who already have advanced qualifications and skills are already convinced of the joy of learning and return for more. The affluent and professional AB classes and the skilled C1s consistently participate more, with the C2s, Ds and Es still believing that they are too old, or 'education's for other people'. Working class older people are most likely to feel alienated by their previous experience of the education system, and to be least confident about their ability or opportunity to return to learning (Carlton and Soulsby, 1999: p.72; see also Ward and Taylor, 1986).

It remains to be observed that in the past, as well as in the present, educational provision has been driven by middle-class notions of what constitutes 'education' (Ward and Taylor, 1986: pp.1-21). As Evans (1985) put it 'we are prisoners of our past'. The nuances that often accompany this type of 'education; (e.g. the language spoken; the type of 'instruction' given etc.) have been those which have always traditionally alienated the working-class, from education. This pretentiousness with which education is enshrined has to be challenged. Education is not a neutral exercise and self-evidently good for all people. It has become both a prisoner and guardian of the dominant ideology and as such is likely to alienate those with little cultural capital as Bourdieu has described it (cited in Gibson, 1986: p.55). For Bourdieu (1974), cultural capital may be contrasted with the notion of economic capital (money, goods etc.). Not everyone possesses economic capital, but everyone posses cultural capital: language, meanings, thought, behavioural styles, values and dispositions. Bourdieu's view is that education always favours a certain kind of cultural capital: that of the dominant culture. Bourdieu's thesis draws our attention to the subtle ways in which 'culture' has worked to reproduce dominant forms of power relationships. It comes very close to Gramsci's concept of *hegemony* also.

Critical educational gerontology and critical gerogogy

It is then increasingly clear that we need to create a new discourse about education for older people. It is our view that this discourse needs to be through critical educational gerontology (CEG). By employing critical theory we may elucidate a set of principles which embrace the empowering and liberating nature of CEG, which in turn provides a deeper awareness of the content and purpose of education for older people.

Such a discourse could be grounded in the work of theorists such as Freire, Gramsci, Bourdieu, Phillipson and others. Their ideas help us to see how we might begin to transform third age education into a more liberating and emancipatory and CEG can show is that the notion of hegemony importantly explains how instrumental rationality and liberal ideology tend to be the dominating principles which are currently driving contemporary third age educational provision.

With this established, we might proceed to develop a concept of critical gerogogy (CG) as the praxis for third age education. As long ago as 1987, Battersby was arguing that gerogogical principles should be predicated on known theories and concepts and he suggested that we could construct a model for gerogogy which drew together research and theory in relation to (a) human development; (b) the teaching of older adults and the ways in which facilitators can become autonomous learners themselves (Evans, 1985); (c) the learning of older adults themselves. He went on to suggest that gerogogy had not been developed theoretically because it had become confused with Knowles's concept of andragogy and those adult educators who have argued that andragogy was not so much a descriptive way of guiding learning and teaching as a philosophical statement which was not based on a carefully argued philosophical context (Battersby, 1987: p.8). Battersby returned to this theme some years later arguing that the conventional paradigm had never allowed the voices of older learners and those educators who worked with them to be heard. In saying this he invoked Schon's work on the 'reflective practitioner', commenting:

What is missing from the literature in educational gerontology, and in the philosophising about the competing paradigms in the field are narratives from educators working with older adults, reflecting on the appropriateness of the content, the strategies and the social and political contexts of education in later life (Battersby, 1993: p.22).

Battersby neatly summarised a paper by Smyth (1992) on teaching and the politics of reflection, which provides some strategies to help educators to develop narratives about their own reflection-in-action:

1   Describe - What do I do? Reflections can be systematically recorded by use of a diary, tape recorder etc.

2   Inform - How am I informed in what I do? When educators begin to describe what they do, they begin to uncover rationales and justifications for their practice. Through discussion with others and/or individual reflection they can begin to see why they operate in the way that they do and how they can move towards change.

3   Confront - Why do I do the things I do?

4   Reconstruct - How might I do things differently? What do I do? How am I informed in what I do? Answers to such questions could help practitioners to understand why they should begin to jettison some of their practices and rituals which may be reinforcing the oppressive view that they know what is best for those with whom they are working in learning groups.

Central to CEG is the recognition that education is not a neutral exercise and that it involves ethical and moral dimensions. Elmore writes eloquently of this in chapter five, this volume. It is our belief that the application of critical theory would lead to those facilitating educational opportunities for older people becoming far more sensitive to a raft of questions, which have already been raised in this chapter as a result of clarifications that have been offered over the years by Battersby (1987, 1993), Schon (1983), Gibson (1986), Smyth (1992) and others. Questions like: Where do the ideas embodied in my work come from? How did I come to adopt them? Whose interests do they serve? What are the power relationships involved in my work? How do they influence my relationships with older people?

Remarkably little has been published on these issues in spite of the fact that ten years ago Percy wrote: 'Gerogogy should be crucially concerned with assisting older people to exploit and to understand their own experience and that of others' (Percy, 1990: p.237).

It is beyond the scope of this volume to examine and develop these ideas in greater detail. But what is very much required is for someone to develop them further. This can only be achieved when practitioners share their experiences in professional practice and here, we are, regrettably in unknown territory.

3 Critical and educational gerontology: relationships and future developments

Chris Phillipson

Introduction

During the 1990s, a number of elements emerged in the growing debate about the nature of an ageing society. First, the continuation of political economy perspectives, these arising through the work of Estes (1979), Walker (1981), Guillemard (1986), and others (see Minkler and Estes, 1992 and 1998; Estes, 1993; Phillipson, 1998, for reviews of this area).[1]

A second area arose from the consolidation of perspectives from the humanities, with important contributions from scholars such as Thomas Cole, Harry Moody, Andrew Achenbaum, and others. Some of the key contributors in this tradition were brought together in a number of volumes published in the early 1990s, these combining the work of historians, ethicists, and other scientists (see, especially, Cole, Van Tassell and Kastenbaum, 1992; Cole et al. 1993; Schaie and Achenbaum, 1993; Bengston and Achenbaum, 1993).

A third influence was that of biographical and narrative perspectives in gerontology, these building on the work of Malcolm Johnson (1976) and Jaber Gubrium (1986). Advocates of this approach have made important contributions to critical gerontology (see, for example, Gubrium, 1993), as well as extending knowledge about the social construction of later life (Ruth and Keynon, 1996).

Taken together, these intellectual trends may be seen as illustrating the emergence of a critical as opposed to traditional gerontology (Baars, 1991; Phillipson and Walker, 1987). The critical elements in this gerontology centre around a number of elements: from political economy, there is awareness of the structural pressures and constraints affecting older people, with divisions associated with class, gender and ethnicity being emphasised (Estes, 1993). From both a humanistic as well as a biographically-orientated gerontology, there is concern over the absence of meaning in the lives of older people, and the sense of doubt and uncertainty which is seen to pervade their daily routines and relationships (Moody, 1992). Finally, from all three perspectives there is a focus on the issue of empowerment, through the transformation of society (for example, through the re-distribution of income and wealth), or the development of new rituals and symbols to facilitate changes though the life course (Kaminksy, 1993).

Critical gerontology in fact draws on a variety of intellectual traditions, these including: Marx's critique of political economy; the Frankfurt School (Adorno, Horkheimer and Marcuse), and more recent researchers from this tradition such as Jurgen Habermas (1971; Moody, 1992); psychoanalytic perspectives (Biggs, 1997); as well as contemporary sociological theorists such as Anthony Giddens (1991). These different approaches are used both to challenge traditional perspectives within gerontology, and to develop an alternative approach to understanding the process of growing old.

Central to the idea of a critical gerontology is the idea of ageing as a socially constructed event. In respect of political economy, this is seen to reflect the role of elements such as the state and economy in influencing the experience of ageing. In relation to the humanities, the role of the individual actively constructing his or her world is emphasised, with biographical approaches emphasising an interplay between the self and society (Keynon, 1996). The idea of *lives* as socially constructed is perhaps the key theme in the approach of critical gerontology, with different points of emphasis depending on the approach taken.

The emergence of critical perspectives has certainly been influential in a number of debates in the field of educational gerontology. Glendenning (1991), for example, has developed the idea of a 'critical educational gerontology', in a review essay in *Ageing and Society*. Glendenning (1991: pp.215-16) sees the role of this new kind of gerontology as follows:

> Critical educational gerontology would encourage tutors and students to examine the relation between knowledge and power and control. It would enable education to be seen as an agent of social change, as it was by the early exponents of the University of the Third Age in France. It would take into account the conflicting messages that we receive about the learning characteristics of older people. We also need clear answers to a number of questions. Among them are: Whose interests are being served? Why do we need education for older adults? ... Should we not be questioning existing practices and models of education for older adults or are we content?

These questions are clearly of great significance and certainly deserve a considered response. However, underpinning the concerns raised is another more fundamental issue, one which Glendenning identified in his paper and some thought to which will be given in this contribution. Essentially, this concerns the question of just what it is that 'older adults experience as they pass through the Third Age' (Glendenning, 1991: p.211). From this one might also ask: how is experience changing in the light of wider transformations within society? How might this influence the role and perspective of critical gerontology? For the remainder of this paper, different aspects of these questions will be reviewed and some issues raised for practice within educational gerontology.

Critical gerontology and the crisis of old age

The starting point for this paper is that it is helpful to see critical gerontology as a response to three different kinds of crisis within the field of ageing. First, there is a distributional crisis, reflected in the economic recession affecting capitalist economies in the 1980s and 1990s. (This is considered in some detail by political economy analysts).

Second, there is a crisis within gerontology, with the attack by Moody, Cole and others, on what they refer to as *instrumental gerontology*. Social gerontology, according to this view, is dominated by a form of rationality which seeks to objectify what is essentially a human and subjective experience (Moody, 1992). Ageing, it is suggested, has been presented as a technical (rather than existential) problem, one which simply needs more and better kinds of scientific intervention. Humanistic perspectives in social gerontology offer a challenge to this traditional approach.

Third, there is the crisis in meaning for older people themselves, this arising, in part, through the uncertainty of society about how to handle ageing populations; in part, also, because of some of the social instabilities associated with what has been termed 'late modern' or 'postmodern societies' (Giddens, 1991; Phillipson, 1998).

The interaction between these three levels is raising profound issues about how best to move forward within gerontology in general, and educational gerontology in particular. The disciplines are, it might be argued, facing difficult problems at the present time, and part of the task must be to provide some broader assessment which might give appropriate clues as to the best way to develop future perspectives. The bulk of this paper is, then, an attempt to provide a commentary on this context, but especially from the standpoint of this issue of 'how the third age is experienced'; and what might be the response of educational gerontology to this experience.

Old age and the life course

The argument being put forward is that we have reached a new crisis in terms of the way in which old age is positioned and handled within the life course. The steady growth in the proportion of older people in the population was, up until the beginning of the 1980s, contained within the dual institutions of retirement and the welfare state (Phillipson, 1998). These created a social, economic and moral space within which growing numbers of people could be channelled. Despite initial resistance (as illustrated by the early post-war literature on attitudes to retirement), the basic social arrangement achieved a considerable degree of acceptance: namely, the idea of a period of active retirement, followed by entry into a period of late old age with the support of an expanding welfare state.

In terms of a cultural history of ageing, this could be said to resolve what remained as an area of ambiguity within society - namely that whilst more older people could be seen as a sign of a mature and prosperous society, 'too many' could also be seen as a burden ('passengers' rather than 'crew' as Robert Ensor (1950) put it, writing in the early 1950s). For a period of at least 20 years, moving older people into the zone of retirement and the welfare state, buttressed as well by the idea of inter-generational support, held at bay the underlying issue of finding a place and identity for older people. In this sense, economics came to the rescue of demographics in the 1950s. The prevailing view, after the flurry of concern around the Royal Commission of Population in 1949, and the Phillips Committee in 1954, was that the problems of older people had been largely resolved - notably in relation to pensions and health. True, the issue of loneliness was discussed in numerous research reports, most notably by Townsend in the 1950s and Tunstall in the 1960s, but the assumption was that these problems could be resolved by reforms to the relationships surrounding work, retirement and the welfare state. Certainly, the fixed point of discussion was that the meaning of old age was to be constructed out of the evolving institution of retirement on the one side, and the mature welfare state on the other: the family providing an essential link between the two.

The unravelling of these arrangements has exposed once again the cultural uncertainties which surround old age. Society is beset, as it was in the 1930s and 1940s (Phillipson, 1982), with anxieties about the most appropriate way to respond to an ageing population. But these uncertainties are given a particular emphasis by the pressures and insecurities associated with a postmodern age. Arguably, older people have been the group with the most to lose with the break-up of the relationships associated with what Lash and Urry (1987) refer to as 'organised capitalism'. For them, the extension of individualization in the period of 'disorganised capitalism', poses a significant threat to identity itself. As Biggs (1993) notes, modern life raises at least two possibilities: the promise of a multiplicity of identities on the one side, the danger of psychological disintegration on the other. Biggs suggests that in response to these circumstances, individual actors will attempt to find socially constructed spaces that lend some form of predictability to everyday relationships. Yet in a postmodern world such spaces may be increasingly difficult to locate.[2] This point has been powerfully made by Zigmunt Baumann (1992) in his book *Postmodernity and its Discontents*. He argues here:

> In our postmodern times ... the boundaries which tend to be simultaneously most strongly desired and most acutely missed are those of a rightful and secure place in society, of a space unquestionably one's own, where one can plan one's life with the minimum of interference, play one's role in a game in which the rules do not change overnight and without notice, and reasonably hope for the better ... It is the widespread characteristic of men and women in our type of society that they live perpetually with the 'identity problem' unresolved. They suffer, one might say, from a chronic absence of resources with which they could build a truly solid and lasting identity, anchor it and stop it from drifting.

In the case of older people, 'identity problems' have always been a significant issue in societies where issues relating to production and reproduction have traditionally been central both to the social order and to the individual's identity within it. Leonard (1984) makes the point that ideological discourse is directed, from childhood onwards, to the performance of productive and reproductive roles which gendered class subjects are expected to perform. Leonard (1984: p.181) concludes that:

> Familial ideology is especially significant in constructing a self which is congruent with dominant conceptions of the activities and capacities involved in present or future roles: mother, father, bread-winner, 'attractive young woman', 'useful member of society' and others. But what happens to those who do don't appear to occupy these central roles? What is the effect of [the experience] of marginality on personality?

In fact, as Leonard (1984) went on to describe, there was a significant literature dealing with the crisis affecting groups such as the working-class elderly and the unemployed, when confronted with the absence of full-time wage labour. On the other hand, it is equally the case that older people have not been passive in their response to mandatory retirement. Although theoretical perspectives such as 'structured dependency theory' (Townsend, 1981) have tended to emphasise a view of older people as victims, an alternative reading would stress the existence of social movements amongst the old in areas such as education, politics and the voluntary sector. However, it can be argued that these movements were built around the notion of a traditional welfare state, with the gradual evolution of retirement (after a lifetime of work) a central element. The problem of marginality raised by Leonard was thus resolved by elevating retirement into a status which would equal that associated with work (a particular concern of course of the pre-retirement movement).

The issue of identity

From the 1980s onwards, the crisis affecting retirement illustrated the way which the problem of social marginality amongst the old had been contained rather than resolved in the post-war period. Moreover, what a postmodern setting did have to offer - namely the ideal of consumption - seemed only to further marginalise groups such as older people. Baumann (1992: p.111), for example, writes of the accelerating emancipation of capital from labour producing a situation where: 'instead of engaging the rest of society in the role of producers, capital tends to engage them in the role of consumers'. But for the majority of the old, the engagement with society was increasingly neither that of producer nor consumer. At the same time, the role of the old as 'icons' of the welfare state, the one group with an inalienable right to whatever services were on offer, was also under attack. Younger generations, it was to be argued were now challenging the traditional view about the 'interdependence' of generations; increasingly generations were seen as contestants for a diminishing welfare pie (a logical outcome, it might be argued, from the individualisation of daily life in a postmodern setting).

These developments have not gone unchallenged but they have confirmed the seriousness of the challenge facing older people. In reality, in terms of their social position, they have moved into a new zone of indeterminacy, marginal to both work and welfare. Older people experience the world truly as though they were riding (as Giddens, 1991, puts it in his description of high modernity) a 'juggernaut': 'It is not just that more or less continuous and profound processes of change occur; rather, change does not consistently conform either to human expectation, or to human control'. This may seem a relatively abstract description of the crisis which older people may experience but it also accurately conveys the reality of what may happen to elderly people placed in situations of rapid change.

The above point can be graphically illustrated with the following example: In April 1997 seven elderly patients died within days of being moved from a mental hospital (which was being closed) to a community care home. The seven people, who had an average age of 80 and were suffering from dementia, are believed to have died from bronchial pneumonia. The manager for the home which received the patients noting the frail condition of the people concerned, commented: 'It is sadly not uncommon for a higher than normal mortality rate to occur in the week after the transfer of patients from a long-stay hospital to a new living environment' (*The Observer*, 27 April 1997).

The manager's point has some validity and is supported by a substantial research literature. On the other hand, it is equally valid to suggest that the situation may not simply be a problem of frailty alone - the fact that five of the seven died virtually within a twenty-four hour period suggests something else may be at work here. The 'something else' that could be affecting the situation may be precisely the issue raised in much of the literature on the changes which beset modern life, namely, to repeat Baumann's point, the extent to which we are no longer sure of a rightful and secure position in the world in which we live. This is important for all of us: young and fit; frail and demented. We all want some sort of anchorage of our identity, to help us explore and make sense of the world. The point that needs to be made here, however, is that in the case of older people, the conditions for securing identity have been drastically changed over the past twenty years. Securing a secure sense of self has become of the biggest challenges in late life: the postmodern self is one riven by insecurity and this is especially the case in the period defined as older age. The central argument of put forward in this paper is that whilst providing the basis -through changes to patterns of fertility and mortality- for developing an ageing society, we seem to have undercut a language and moral space which can resonate with the rights and needs of older people as a group.

This is a large statement and needs much justification if it is not to seem overly simplistic and facile. To put some flesh on the argument, I want to explore a particular approach to the construction of the self, and then in discussion perhaps review the implications for educational gerontology.

The self in old age

Asking questions about the status of the self in old age remains difficult, given the absence of a strong and clearly-defined research tradition in this area. But asking questions about the status of selfhood in late life is fundamental to any understanding of the problems facing older people. To illustrate these issues, some of the arguments developed in Charles Taylor's (1989) important study *Sources of the Self* will now be discussed, and in particular their relevance in terms of position of older people. Taylor's concern in his study is to explore the basis of what he terms as the 'modern identity'. Essentially, this involves him tracing 'various strands of our modern notion of what it is to be a human agent, a person, or a self' (Taylor, 1989: p.3). A central concern of this book is that the frameworks within which people have been traditionally anchored, have been made problematic within the modern world. Philosophical or theological doctrines, at least in the Western world, no longer have a the binding force on people's consciousness, that was once the case. Such doctrines do not 'form the horizon' of the whole society in the modern western world (Taylor, 1989). The consequence of the this is the crisis of meaning which we now associate as a fundamental condition of living in a modern and postmodern world. At its most extreme, this crisis of meaning confronts the modern individual as a condition in which: 'the world loses altogether its spiritual contour, nothing is worth doing, the fear is of a terrifying emptiness, a kind of vertigo, or even a fracturing of our world and body-space' (Taylor, 1989: p.18).

Perhaps something of this kind gripped the demented souls described earlier. But the condition itself is viewed as general to man/woman in the western world; a feature of the crisis which is seen to grip the modern identity faced with the dominance of what some would describe as 'instrumental rationality'. Taylor's (1989) essential point though is that living without a framework (or moral sources) for our lives is an impossibility, for the following reasons:

Frameworks provide the background, explicit or implicit, for our moral judgements, intuitions, or responses ... To articulate a framework is to explicate what makes sense of our moral responses. That is, when we try to spell out what it is that we presuppose when we judge that a certain form of life is truly worthwhile, or place our dignity in a certain achievement or status, or define our moral obligations in a certain manner, we find ourselves articulating inter alia what I have been calling here 'frameworks'.

Taylor goes on to argue:

I want to defend the strong thesis that doing without frameworks is utterly impossible for us; otherwise put, that the horizons within which we live our lives and which make sense of them have to include these qualitative distinctions. Moreover, this is not meant just as a contingently true psychological fact about human beings, which could perhaps turn out one day not to hold for some exceptional individual ... Rather, the claim is that living within such strongly qualified horizons is constitutive of human agency, that stepping outside these limits would be tantamount to stepping outside what we would recognise as integral, that is, undamaged human personhood.

From this, Taylor draws out the following conclusion:

Perhaps the best way to see this is to focus on the issue that we usually describe today as the issue of identity. We speak of it in these terms because the question is often spontaneously phrased by people in the form: who am I? But this can't necessarily be answered by giving name and genealogy. What

32

does answer this question for us is an understanding of what is of crucial importance to us. To know who I am is a species of knowing where I stand. My identity is defined by the commitments and identification which provide the frame or horizon within which I try to determine from case to case what is good, or valuable, or what ought to be done, or what I endorse or oppose. In other words, it is the horizon within which I am capable of making a stand.

For Taylor, a crisis of identity occurs in situations where individuals are uncertain of their position in the world. They lack a framework within which day to living assumes a stable significance; the available options seem to lack meaning and substance. People enter a world where the possibilities before them appear unfixed and undetermined. Taylor concludes that: 'This is a painful and frightening experience'.

The above analysis is a powerful statement of the existential doubts (and nightmares) which often seem to beset older people. Where do they stand in a world in which priorities and values are constantly open to revision and change? What is the moral and existential space to which they are entitled, in a world where social integration is achieved through the operation of the marketplace?

This is not, it should be noted, a rehearsal of an old argument that the problem facing older people is that they lack meaningful roles which tie them to society (a perspective which was influential in sociological thinking about older people in the 1950s and 1960s). Rather, there is a much harder argument here: namely, that modern living undercuts the construction of a viable identity for living in old age. To be sure, the idea of older people as a marginal group is not new, and has been debated within critical gerontology for a number of years. But the argument being developed is that marginality is now being experienced in a new and somewhat distinctive way by older people. Marginality, for much of the post-war period, could, it is argued, be re-claimed through identities constructed out of an emerging consensus regarding retirement and welfare state. The collapse of this consensus has exposed once again the vulnerable status of the old. But this vulnerability is not just about the material experience of deprivation, it also reaches into the experience of day-to-day life. People now find themselves exposed to situations where they seem to lack identity: 'Who am I?', has become a difficult question for many to answer. For the seven 'frail' older people in a north London care home, few people could provide any answers -least of all those concerned with actually running the service. But in society as a whole -moving into a new century- the idea of an ageing population seems increasingly to offer dubious benefits. In sacrificing one set of institutions for supporting old age, we have left open their replacement.

Emancipation and the role of educational gerontology

The social vacuum facing some groups of older people seems to me to be one of enormous danger. Developing an effective response to this must involve an important role for those concerned with educational gerontology. In this respect, educational gerontology needs to place itself squarely within the humanistic 'turn' within gerontology which has emerged over the past decade. In particular, that element within critical gerontology which has reinserted the notion of ageing as a 'lived experience', one which demands a dialogue between the older person, the academic community, practitioners, as well as other relevant groups.

Harry Moody, in developing this work, suggests however that critical gerontology must go beyond merely a negative critique of current practice and ideology, offering as well its own vision of a different approach. Accordingly:

> A critical gerontology must also offer a positive idea of human development:
> that is, aging as movement toward freedom beyond domination (autonomy,
> wisdom, transcendence). Without this emancipatory discourse (i.e. an
> expanded image of aging) we have no means to orient ourselves in struggling
> against current forms of domination.

Moody (1982) calls in fact for an emancipatory praxis (or practice) which can transcend the conventional categories of work, sex roles and age stereotypes. These are seen to circumscribe the possibilities of human development, and to produce a 'shrunken and fragmented view of what the life course might be' (Moody, 1982: p.35). The great challenge at the present is to redraw our perspective on the life course, and how older age is constructed within it. From this view, educational gerontology must be a mainstream element within critical perspectives, contributing to the debate on how we close what seems to be an alarming and somewhat alienating gap: the disjunction between ourselves as we age from within, and ourselves as we age within society.

An important source for reconstructing the basis for older age must also be located within the field of education and learning. The relevance of this has to be placed in the context of the neglect of older adults within the educational system. The most authoritative estimates here - for Britain at least - have been produced by Schuller and Bostyn (1992), in their report for the Carnegie Inquiry into the Third Age. They estimated a figure of three quarter of a million people in the 50-74 age group enrolled annually in some kind of formal adult education, with a similar number receiving some kind of organised training. Applying this level of participation to the total number of people 50 plus in the UK, means that roughly 1 in 10 of the age group take part each year in formal learning. An equivalent number - and probably rather more - engage in informal learning, that is activities which involve an intention to learn but which are not formally designated as such.

The international evidence is summarised by Schuller and Bostyn (1992: p.9) as follows:

> No country appears outstanding in its educational provision specifically for older people, although the United States can claim to have pioneered interesting initiatives ... and to have witnessed the strongest anti-discrimination statements. There are certain areas in which the UK can claim to be reasonable advanced, for example with the Open University and community education. Against this must be set the great overall deficit in the initial and continuing education and training of the population as a whole, now documented in numerous analyses. the contrast is sharpest with countries such as Scandinavia, where participation in adult education so much more firmly part of the culture, with participation rates of 23 per cent and 16 per cent recorded for the 60-64 and 65-74 age groups in [the early 1980s].

The fact that nine out of ten older people in Britain are disengaged from formal learning raises major issues about inequities in the distribution of educational resources. The figure is skewed to some extent by cohort factors, in particular (as Schuller and Bostyn highlight) the fact that two out of three of those aged 50 and over left school at 15 and over. However, additional factors must include negative stereotypes about older people as potential learners; the impact of poverty and social class; and, as well, failure to develop education as a social right to be available throughout the life course. The last of these existing despite the urging of UNESCO (in the 1970s) for lifelong learning, on the grounds that this would:

> ... enable those who had left working life to retain their physical and intellectual faculties and to continue to participate in community life and also to give them access to fields which have not been open to them during their working life (cited in Glendenning, 1990: p.14).

In fact, the reality of the decades of the 1980s and 1990s was that, despite the expansion in the number of retirees, educational opportunities for older people were significantly reduced. Evidence for this can be found in the 1999 survey of participation in adult education commissioned by the National Institute for Adult Continuing Education (NIACE), which compared trends since the last national survey in 1996. On the basis of the figures presented, older people would appear to have lost ground over this period, with a 20 per cent drop in participation during the three years.[3] As Tuckett (1999) argues, the crisis in the university adult education sector has had a disproportionate impact on older people, who comprise the largest group attending day and evening classes. Community education organised by local government has, historically, been a major provider of education for older people. Once again, this sector has faced contraction in its range of provision, despite the expansion in the numbers of potential participants. This contradiction has also been massively apparent in the 'cinderella area' of pre-retirement education (PRE). Despite the publication of national surveys in the early 1980s urging improvement in terms of the quality and take-up of programmes (Coleman, 1983; Phillipson and Strang, 1983), there was almost certainly a decline during the 1980s in the numbers participating in PRE. Schuller and Bostyn (1992: p.20) calculate a figure of 30, 000 people participating annually in PRE, a derisory figure given the approximately 600,000 people in the cohort five years below state retirement age.

Taken overall, the figures highlighted above represent a massive exclusion of older people from learning opportunities which might add substantially to quality of the twenty or more years spent in retirement. Given the chronic employment problems in the late 1970s and through the 1980s, governments were content to expand the number of retirees. At the same time, as we have seen, access to education programmes was reduced, and even the modest programmes to help people prepare for retirement were cut back.

Faced with this situation, it seems important to argue for a fresh perspective on the importance of older learners, both to society and the economy. In respect of Government responsibilities, some of the key policy issues have been summarised by Schuller and Bostyn (1992: p.98) as follows:

[First] A clear policy statement on the rights of older people to a broad range of educational opportunity. [Second] All relevant educational bodies to have a clear obligation towards adult learners, including older adults. [Third] the duty on local education authorities to secure sufficient provision of adult education to be confirmed, accompanied by adequate resources. [Fourth] coordination of and support for distance learning providers, with particular reference to older learners with problems of mobility.

These, and the many other policy proposals raised by these researchers, should be seen as a national priority.[4] It would be an exaggeration to argue that without effective education provision, the years in retirement are wasted. Older people have, in fact, been highly successful in promoting diverse and imaginative educational activities of their own. But there is a massive case for expanding the field, and drawing on the resources of older people in different ways throughout the community. More fundamentally, perspectives from critical gerontology would suggest that education can play a major role in re-defining the place of older people within the life course. Here, the issue of securing a sense of place and identity in a 'postmodern' world has become one of great significance for older people. The future of educational gerontology must lie in acknowledging what are fundamental changes to the sociological context within which old age operates:

this may be seen as representing a unique challenge to the educational field but one to which it should certainly make a vigorous and positive response.

Notes

1 The volume by Minkler and Estes (1997) provides a review of some of the issues identified here.
2 The work of Biggs (1993; 1997) has been important in developing an approach to understanding the nature of selfhood in old age.
3 In the 65-74 age group in 1999, 16 per cent of those surveyed had been active in some form of learning at some point over a three year period; this compared with 19 per cent in 1996; the equivalent figures for the 75 plus group were 9 and 15 per cent (Tuckett, 1999).
4 See, for example, Carlton and Soulsby (1999).

4 Changing attitudes to ageing

There are many derogatory stereotypes of older people: 'senile', 'wrinkly', 'oldie', 'geriatric'. But as Norman pointed out in her paper on ageism, 'we don't call a sick child a paediatric, or a woman having a hysterectomy, an 'obstetric'. She went further saying that terms like 'old folks' and 'old girls' were invariably infantilising (Norman, 1987: p.4; see also Featherstone and Hepworth, 1993: p.308).

Poverty and enfeeblement

In the twentieth century there has been a recurrent negative theme about old age and it has a long pedigree. One of the popular myths of the past was that elderly people who were without means ended their days in the workhouse (Thomson, 1983: p.44). This fear was an over-simplification of history. While the workhouse was synonymous with poverty and is painfully ingrained in the British collective memory, poverty itself is not a myth.

In the middle of the nineteenth century between half and three quarters of all English women over 70 received a weekly Poor Law allowance of 2s 3d to 3s. Elderly women were not expected to have their own financial resources. Elderly men were treated less kindly. All men over 67 were expected to be in work and capable of making their own living, but over 70, relief was available and between a quarter and a half of all men over 70 in England received it. By 1894, when Charles Booth published his survey of the aged poor, a third of those over 70 were compelled to seek Poor Law relief (Norton, 1990: p.15). Nearly a century later, the government's Family Expenditure Survey (1992) showed that retired households (however that is defined), depended on social security benefits for 41 per cent of household income in contrast to 11 per cent for all households (Oppenheim, 1993: p.68). So what has changed?

Poverty

'Poverty' is most often defined as a threshold which corresponds to a minimum acceptable standard of living and by 'poor' is meant those whose incomes fall below the level of Income Supplement. By 1987, 31 per cent of the poor were elderly (Seaton and Hancock, 1995: pp.2-3). We may go further by adding that the majority of those living 'on the margins of poverty are lone elderly women' (Groves, 1993: 54; see also Arber and Ginn, 1991 and Whittaker, 1997).

For the majority, old age has always been equated with poverty and feared because of the massive shame and resentment it will bring. A current example of social tragedy is that because of this learnt stereotype, 880,000 pensioners in Britain are entitled to income support, but are not claiming it according to recent estimates from the Department of Social Security. The amount unclaimed is worth £705 million (Hansard, 19/10/98 col.37, 1998). The inequality of this situation is that the UK Treasury is profiting from the embarrassment and suffering of these older people. An important aspect of the development of this stereotype has been the correlation between work and productivity, with the consequent notion that older people are unproductive. Until the middle of the twentieth century most men worked until they died. Phillipson has estimated that at the time of the Old Age Pensions Bill in 1908, 606 out of every 1,000 men were still working (Phillipson, 1977: p.15). In the parliamentary debate on pensions Lloyd George argued in favour of the pension being given at 65, saying that between 65 and 70 the test for continued employment was to be 'infirmity' and 'the question of the broken down old man of 67 and 68 who is left to charity' (Phillipson, *ibid.*). Phillipson comments that the very term 'broken down old man' reflects a historical tradition of identifying the retired working class male as useless, worn out and unemployable, to be grouped with the infirm and feeble minded as a category in social policy. The establishment of the stereotype of old age as 'enfeeblement' had by now been established. This was further compounded when the Pensions Act became law on 1 January 1909. Pensions would be withheld from those who had failed to work habitually according to their ability and need, and those who had failed to save money regularly. Here wrote Roberts was a means test with a vengeance. Paupers were not entitled to any pension (Roberts, 1978: p.84).

By the mid-1950s, it was being argued in social medicine that retirement was detrimental to health and this pessimism came together with the notion of enfeeblement and the constant fear of poverty in old age (Phillipson, 1992: p.28), which was by now deeply engrained in the collective memory. Indeed the retirement pension has been steadily eroded as a proportion of average male

s since 1979, when it became related to price increases rather than to
, as had previously been the case. By 1992, the pension for a single
as equivalent to 17.8 per cent of average male earnings.

with this background, we have been subjected to uncritical generalisations from politicians who have described the ageing population as a 'burden', a 'danger', and a 'demographic time bomb'. Add to this then the effect of the dominant biomedical model that older age is a process of inevitable decline and we begin to see how the concept of 'ageism' has come about, with the implication that there is 'a process of systematic stereotyping of and discrimination against people because they are old, just as racism and sexism accomplish this for skin colour and gender' (Butler and Lewis, 1982: p.176).

Butler, an internationally respected American psychiatrist expanded on this some years later:

> Ageism, the prejudice of one group against another, has been applied mostly to the prejudice of younger people toward older people. Underlying ageism is the awesome dread and fear of growing older, and therefore the desire to distance ourselves from older persons who are a proxy portrait for our future selves. We see the young dreading ageing and the old envying youth. Ageism not only reduces the status of older people but of all people (Butler, 1986: p.12).

Myths and stereotypes

In 1975, in a book which won him the Pulitzer Prize, Butler wrote about the myths and stereotypes about the old. Many current views of older people represent confusions, misunderstandings and lack of knowledge about old age. The concept of chronological age (measuring age by the number of years one has lived) is a kind of myth, because as Butler claims, physiological indicators show a greater range in old age than in other age groups, and this he says is true of personality as well. In his book he charts a number of myths about old age (Butler, 1975: pp.6-16):

1. *The myth of unproductivity* is a myth because countless people become unusually creative for the first time when they are older.

2. *The myth of disengagement* (which gained great currency in the 1960s as a result of a book by Cumming and Henry (*Growing Old*, 1966). The myth that

after retirement, older people prefer to disengage from activities in society and that this is a natural part of the ageing experience. But there is no evidence to support this theory and disengagement is only one reaction to growing old. What is more, the concept of 'retirement' from paid work is becoming a myth in the post-industrial world of the late twentieth century. There are increasingly fewer jobs to retire from if you are over 45 or 50. The disengagement theory was in effect functional because it encouraged younger people to take over older people's practical roles.

3. *The myth of inflexibility* which has little to do with age and more to do with character formation.

4. *The myth of senility* is the notion that older people are forgetful, with confusional episodes and reduced attention, is a popular view held both inside and outside the medical profession, in an attempt to categorise the behaviour of older people. But there is often confusion between brain damage and other mental and emotional problems in later life. Depression and anxiety, for example, are treatable and often reversible. Irreversible brain damage such as senile dementia of the Alzheimer type is of course not a myth. The use of the word 'senile' is usually an inaccurate diagnostic label and should be avoided, just as we should avoid regarding older people as a homogeneous mass. Each person is different and unique.

5. *The myth of serenity* which portrays old age as an adult fairyland enjoying peace, relaxation and serenity. But as Butler observes, older people experience more stresses than any other age group, with depression, anxiety anger, chronic discomfort, grief, isolation and lowered esteem.

These attitudes and myths are very old and lodged in the folk memory of western society.

Cognitive decline

Another point of great importance and of special relevance to this volume is the popular misconception that cognitive decline is inevitable as we grow older. H.C. Lehmann wrote the classic text *Age and Achievement* between 1928 and 1953. It was written during the booming modernizing years to inform education and training policies how the development of knowledge and skills is affected by age. He deduced from his research that the highest output was between 30 and 34 and he showed that the peak years of established leadership were between 50 and 70, whereas in sport the peak years were between 20 and 40. Lehmann maintained that after 34 output fell steadily until 49, when it was less than half the output 15 years earlier and was nearly at zero (Bromley, 1988).

Bytheway in his monograph on ageism discusses the question 'How important have these kind of claims been in setting the basis for age prejudice?' (Bytheway, 1995: p.24). Since the 1960s, much more research has been done, particularly in the USA. The Americans were fortunate that several lifespan developmental psychologists were able to obtain funding for longitudinal surveys and an evaluation of ageing. The most famous of which, was established in Seattle in 1956. There are also important studies in Baltimore, North Carolina and in Europe in Gothenburg, Berlin and Bonn. The evidence that is emerging is that only a small proportion of physical decrements in old age can be adduced to inevitable physiological deterioration, and that it is the duration and intensity of training and physical activity which to a large degree determines the performance of many people as they grow older. After 40 years of measurement the Seattle study is showing that cognitive decline is not inevitable either and that where intellectual decline has been shown to exist, it is possible through carefully planned instruction strategies at the ability level to reverse the process, and although it is not universally true, Warner Schaie and his team have found that '40 per cent of those who declined significantly over 14 years were returned to their pre-decline level' (Schaie, 1990: p.302).

It is therefore unacceptable on the basis of scientifically obtained evidence to maintain that older people enter into intellectual decline as a matter of course. Thus another stereotype about ageing can be rebutted.

Structured dependence

Any serious discussion about ageing must be seen against this complex background and it enables us to realise that old age has been socially constructed, that old people are marginalised, within their structured dependence, a process that has been so thoroughly described in various books and papers by Townsend (1986), Phillipson (1982), Walker (1980, 1983, 1996).

Nevertheless, the result of this process which has been described above is the formation of stereotypes which it is difficult to eradicate from the collective memory. Given the centuries' old background of stereotypes and attitudes towards old people and given that so many older people are trapped within their own models of ageing which are ultimately unacceptable to those who share a positive view of ageing, it is not difficult to understand why the stigma of ageing continues to retain a vice-like grip on the public imagination (Hepworth, 1988: p.16).

However there are two interesting factors at play. The first is the surge of positive thinking about growing older, which has emerged from developments in gerontology, health and social welfare in the last 25 years, when it came to be realised that differences between individuals related little to age, but much more to factors such as social class, education, health and environment (Glendenning, 1996: p.17). The second is the existence of what we have come to call the 'baby boomers'.

Welfare provision and social policy

Bernard and Phillips have pointed out that the provision of welfare for older people in the 1950s and 1960s had no conceptual framework with no clear direction for social policy, partly because the legacies of the Poor Law persisted well into the 1950s (Bernard and Phillips, 1998: p.6). The 1948 National Assistance Act still saw residential care as the solution to the needs of older people. The concept of community care had been around since the 1940s, but there was a lack of political commitment to its development. This inability to move resulted from the huge resources already committed to residential care. Not only was there substantial capital investment in property, there was also a strong residential care lobby which continued until well into the 1990s, thus guaranteeing that residential care for older people would dominate the history of social welfare and social policy for most of the century. Because there had been little research attention paid to older people in residential care, even after Townsend (1962) and Robb (1967), action was directed at institutions and building regulations rather than individuals and the quality of their care, a situation which continued into the 1970s. Older people were still seen as a dependent group in need of care. By the 1980s, the Audit Commission has produced its formative report which described community care as being 'in disarray' (Audit Commission, 1986).

By the 1990s and the National Health Service and Community Care Act 1990, a new language had emerged (Bernard and Phillips, 1998: p.13). After the rigours of social policy in the 19th century and most of the 20th century, we were now relating the needs of older people themselves to their empowerment and advocacy, user-involvement and participation, care management and packages of care, which were designed to restore to older people a sense of dignity and self-worth, which began by degrees to become part of the common language which was to be increasingly monitored by the media and individual whistle-blowers and pressure groups. But behind the rhetoric and the popular sense of new-found liberation lay what Walker discerned as the continual erosion of state responsibility for the care of older people with a social policy that was imposed from the top down and mainly concerned with cost-containment and management issues (Walker, 1993). In 1995, Higgs suggested that 'rights' all but disappeared as services withdrew further and older people without personal and financial resources were faced with very little choice over their lives (Higgs, 1995). In this sense we may say "What has changed since the last century?" But on the other hand we do not find it difficult to detect a decisive change in the way in which the attitude towards older people has shifted away from that of enfeeblement and lack of worth to a view which is more sociologically based and which requires a much clearer articulation before it can become part of everyday language (Phillipson, 1998).

Additionally, there remain distinct challenges in the realm of social policy which will pursue us well into the 21st century. The book of essays edited by Bernard and Phillips to honour the first fifty years of the Centre for Policy on Ageing (Bernard and Phillips, 1998) provides an excellent starting point for understanding where we are at in social gerontology, a concept undreamt of 150 years ago.

'Baby boomers'

The second factor underlying the changed attitudes about ageing lies in the existence of the 'baby boomers'. Official government projections indicate that by 2026 there will be 17.5 million people in the UK aged 60 or over. Most of this increase is due to the two 'baby booms' of 1946-50 and the early 1960s. Evandrou has pointed out that little attention has been paid to the likely socio-economic characteristics of these baby boom generations and how they may differ from previous groups of older people (Evandrou, 1997: p.8). In the first place, they were born into and grew up in different social, economic and technological climates. People born in the peak year of 1964 were not even old enough to vote when the Thatcher government first came to power. Yet the legacy of Thatcherism and its arguably divisive policies has shaped their adult life.

The differences between the experiences of people born before and after World War II is considerable. The younger ones for example have no experience of war, apart from the Falklands and Gulf wars and the recent war in former Yugoslavia, nor of growing up in the so-called welfare state, reaping the benefits of universal secondary education as a result of the 1944 Education Act and expecting to receive health and social care under the National Health Service and Social Services.

The 'baby boomers' of the 1940s were born in a period of immediate post-war austerity, with food rationing and selective education. However when they entered the labour market, the economy was entering a period of relative stability and the rapid expansion of higher education in the 1960s meant that many of them stayed on at school and entered university. In addition, the introduction of the contraceptive pill ushered in a new sexual freedom. This was a far cry from the experiences of the older generations as described in chapter 1 and earlier in this chapter (Now statistically in either the 'young-old' category or in late old age). This was a period where there were decisive shifts in the balance of power in society. The 1960s witnessed the development of a more open society with the student behaviour and experimentation on an increasing number of campuses, the role of popular music and the popularity of the guitar, the development of the women's movement and a growing awareness of gender issues which led to a greater tolerance between the sexes. Television also played a significant role in the provision of instant national and international information and the provision of new forms of education and debate.

In contrast, the 'baby boomers' of the early 1960s were actually born into a period of relative prosperity, with an emphasis on consumer spending, overseas holidays and comprehensive secondary education. But by the time they came to enter the labour market at the end of the 1970s, the country was entering into economic recession, with a sharp rise in unemployment. Many of this group found it impossible to obtain a full-time job. Many more were experiencing redundancy from their jobs and having to face what came to be termed 'long-term unemployment', with the additional incubus of ageist employment policies and lack of special skills and range of competencies which were now required for the new post-industrial technological society. The experience of openness and radicalism of the previous generation was largely in abeyance. The discovery of AIDS suggested the end of the sexual revolution only to be followed miserably by the drug culture, deeply affecting many of the children of the baby boomers. The emphasis of the New Right on wealth creation and the market economy resulted in the cult of individualism and the abandonment of collectivism, sociologists uncovering layer after layer of society to demonstrate what Walker (1997) has called 'the strategy of inequality' and the development of social exclusion. The last twenty years has seen a dramatic polarisation between rich and poor. This was also contemporaneous with the development of Britain's multi-ethnic society since the late 1940s. Britain is now a society ill-at-ease with itself.

Changing attitudes

The implication of what has gone before in this chapter is that inevitably attitudes to ageing have changed as a result. While some of the negative stereotypes about older people remain, we are witnessing in contemporary British society a wider awareness of the differing implications of growing old and a growing sense of corporate responsibility for elderly people. Witness the continual debate about the problems of long-term care, and the discovery, since the 1980s, that many old people are 'at risk' from abuse and neglect both in institutional and family care (Glendenning, 1997).

On the other hand there are debates about generational equity (Walker, 1996), needs assessment and means testing, the regulation of services, pension provision, health and social welfare for older people (see further Bernard and Phillips, 1998 passim.). It is a debate which Midwinter suggests 'must in all political propriety, assume a civic character, as well as an economic one, it is about the political bottom line being not subsistence, but participation. It is about joining in rather than getting by' (Midwinter, 1997). Featherstone and Hepworth (1989: p.154) have gone further by examining what they call 'the modernisation of ageing', through the development of new more youthful images of retirement which provide a challenge to conventional models of ageing. Allied to this development they describe 'the social construction of middle age' which develops into a period of extended mid-life where we may observe a complex of states of 'being', 'development' and 'personal growth' mediated by *transitional* states of crisis. But as Phillipson comments: 'It may only be the elite and the wealthy who are normally in a position to transgress existing conventions about age or who can afford expensive forms of body maintenance ... For most older people, the negative features of ageing may actually increase' (Phillipson, 1998: p.48).

This perhaps is the very great difference between growing old in post-modern Britain and growing old a century ago. Some older people have begun to be humanised for the first time for many generations, coupled with the growing belief in what Bernard and Phillips have called 'an intergenerational life course perspective' (Bernard and Phillips, 1998: p.294), which implies that we should focus on 'ageing' rather than 'old people' and 'old age', and that ultimately the distinction between the third and fourth age, which we discussed in chapter one is divisive.

Positive approaches to ageing

A great deal is written these days about 'positive approaches to ageing'. Examples abound of older people at leisure, embracing physical activity, sport and outdoor adventure holidays, positive health initiatives, overseas holidays and self-help education. The Carnegie research demonstrated most clearly that the participants in these activities tend to be better educated, better-off and white, thus reinforcing the compelling view of Bernard and Phillips that this contributes to an even greater polarisation and distancing between the third and fourth ages, with those in the fourth age finding themselves ill, sick, impoverished and dependent (Bernard and Phillips, 1998: p.295), thus underscoring the 'the great divide' in society, in health, wealth, education and environment.

A great deal has certainly changed in our attitudes to ageing over the generations that have passed since the Poor Law. But stark realities still remain. Stereotypes still exist, often reinforced unconsciously by those who are engaged in what Estes called 'the ageing enterprise' (1979). She saw the critical need of many older people for long-term care, which was being met in the nursing industry by new, young professionals, who very often without realising it, were adopting a position of colonising the older age group who had become a new class of consumers; colonising rather than standing back, keeping their boundaries open and their professional concerns broad, thus the better able to empower older people to take a greater control of their lives.

The twentieth century had began with the stereotype of old age as 'enfeeblement'. It closes significantly with such slogans as "I'm getting older and bolder", "If you don't want to lose it, use it" and "your age is probably the one thing that is not your fault"! The difference in attitude is striking.

5 Education for older people: the moral dimension

Robert Elmore

Introduction

In this paper an attempt is made is to establish the claim that access to educational gerontology - that is a specific form of education for older people - ought to be accorded a high priority in public policy. It is not an easy task and some might reject the claim precipitately on prejudicial grounds or by reference to social, psychological and economic beliefs which have only a passing acquaintance with reality. Others, I hope, will pursue the argument and at least recognize that there is a genuine claim requiring examination. It is not dissimilar to that advanced for access to some form of health care, though not perhaps with the same degree of necessity but nevertheless, like health care it can offer the possibility of improvement in the quality of life for a significant proportion of the population, many of whom have been disadvantage through no fault of their own. There are two major strands to the claim: one is concerned with the fact that as people age they become increasingly marginalized by society in economic, social, political and cultural terms; and, two, the sheer size of the numbers involved, coupled with the fact that existing disadvantages associated with race, gender and class are exacerbated by those associated with advancing age.

The general approach adopted is broadly based on the discursive method of 'wide reflective equilibrium', the approach described by Rawls (1971) and Daniels (1996). It is not an exhaustive study in this mode; that would require a more comprehensive review than is possible here, but like that approach it draws on both moral and non-moral sources in an attempt to establish a practical ethical approach to the issue.

To focus the discussion an effort will be made to justify the statement that the withholding of access to educational gerontology violates the rights to treatment as an equal, equality of opportunity and reduces the status of older people both as persons and citizens.

Preliminary considerations

In recent decades, fundamental changes in the social and economic structure of contemporary Western society challenge many firmly entrenched values and beliefs engendering a deep sense of personal insecurity. Some have welcomed these changes as a liberating process: others, perhaps more circumspect temper their welcome with a degree of scepticism. These phenomena have been variously characterised as post-Fordism, post-modernism or post-scarcity and vigorous debate continues about the most appropriate way of conceptualising them, or for that matter whether they merely constitute a continuity of earlier trends. This debate will not be pursued here but the phenomena the debate is about form a background to this paper.

What is occurring is a profound revaluation of many of the values, beliefs, attitudes which have been attached to institutions, persons and relationships along with an increasing growth in a moral relativism which broadly places emphasis upon individuality and hedonistic self-fulfilment, to the detriment of notion of civility. Thus, for example, there is a proliferation of varying forms of personal life-styles, domestic arrangements, taste, aesthetics and sexuality. Associated with this is the increasing complexity in the capacity to resolve differences or conflicts because of the wide range of criteria available reflecting different value positions. Thus values, attitude and norms which, at one time, have been central to life and society and which have attracted widespread support may be seen as inappropriate, outmoded, wrong, and sometimes immoral, and need to be revised. Those persons, groups or institutions which fail to adapt in some degree to these new elements are perceived as being irrationally resistant to change. All sections and all levels of society are likely to be affected but perhaps the most vulnerable to this process are older people who experience both a loss of political power and influence, and an increasing inequality in society. The force of this movement has such an imperative that individuals, institutions and society at large have begun to develop a repertory of techniques to contain both the disintegrating elements as well as embracing the fresh opportunities by providing access for the development of those economic, political, social and personal skills for those endeavouring to cope with this seemingly inexorable social force.

These changes, coupled with ageing populations in Europe, North America and Australasia, have increasingly become a focus of concern because of the impact they are likely to have on the level of life satisfaction of older people and to impair their capacity to participate in political and cultural activities. Given the size of the population involved this is not a trivial matter yet in public debate the matter seems to have only a modest priority. Here it is important to stress that the difficulties are generated by social and economic institutions and not simply a consequences of chronological ageing. As Vincent argues:

... to understand the meaning of old age it is necessary to understand the culture in which it is located, and how that culture has developed. If the problem of old age in modern Western society is the loss of meaningful roles for elderly people, then how can this loss of culture meaning be overcome? Growing old cannot be understood apart from its subjective experience, mediated by social conditions and cultural significance. What aspects of modern culture are amenable to reassessment in ways that can help redress the evaluation of old age (Vincent, 1995: p.86).

The crucial role of education

One of the key elements which has been identified as being crucial in enabling people to encompass the pressures of rapid social and economic change is access to comprehensive educational and training opportunities which remain available throughout life. However, older people have only featured at the periphery of any arrangements possibly because the conventional life-course pattern of education, employment and retirement, which is perceived as simply leisure, has been an unseen and pervasive presence in this debate. As a response to this sociologists, gerontologists and especially educational gerontologists have become increasing involved in arguing that education for older people is no less important than for other groups and the fact that some may not be within the remunerated labour market does not invalidate this proposition. It may mean however, that there are special additional factors of an educational nature which can help to enhance their status in contemporary society. Yet despite this interest, in political terms their education is seen simply as an optional addition with a relatively low priority in relation to the allocation of resources.

In an important paper Glendenning speculates about some of the reasons why the study of the education and educationally related needs of older people (educational gerontology) has failed to established itself as a field of study. He writes:

None of my arguments so far answers why educational gerontology is not established as a field of study in the UK. One reason is that the body of knowledge about it has never got beyond the anecdotal. What has never had priority is the exploration with older learner, through the educational process, of the complex forces that have led to older people's marginalisation by society

51

and the structured dependency within which society and poverty has encapsulated so many of them (Glendenning, 1997: p.87).

What might be the reasons for neglect? Some have suggested that elements of prejudice or inaccurate stereotypes have influenced public perceptions of the capacities of older people. Certainly, there would appear to be abundant evidence to support such a claim. If this is really so , there is a case to view educational gerontology as a kind of remedial education which challenges not only those attitudes which deny older people their legitimate rights but corrects any false perceptions that older people may have of themselves. There have been similar responses in relation to sex discrimination and racism.

This paper is a preliminary attempt to present argument which would indicate that concern with the education of older adults in its broadest sense and the education and training of the many professionals whose activities impinge on the lives of older people, is not to be regarded as a peripheral issue or a private matter but rather one which is integral to the values of an open democratic society and essential if the notion of 'social inclusion' is to have action added to the rhetoric of recent years. It unashamedly presents a normative case arguing that in a liberal democratic society the rights, privileges and duties of citizenship which underpin social justice persist throughout life and processes, intended or unintended, which undermine them have to be seen as a violation of these fundamental principles. In this respect education is one of the indispensable tools of liberal democracy.

Older people and education

What kind of education might be especially important for older people and how might it be distinguished from that for other age groups? It is widely accepted that they have special educational needs relating to their position in society and for that reason the term 'educational gerontology' has been used to distinguish it from other forms of education. All that can be done here is briefly to illustrate what it might contain.

Clearly it must have relevance to their current and future experience and offer insights for future generations. As other age groups their learning needs will involve both instrumental and expressive dimensions of life but their needs in both these respects are likely to be significantly different from those of younger age groups. There will clearly be a vocational content for those who wish to enhance their employment possibilities but it is likely to be less urgent in terms of career development though this must not be precluded. Perhaps more importantly, will be the acquisition of skills to enable them to continue to contribute as full members of the community and to combat the hardly articulated, but widely pervasive view that older people, in general, ought to be more passive participants in economic, political and community life and perhaps play a less active role. Retirement can be a significantly disempowering and stigmatizing experience and maintaining economic, social and political status from a different social and economic location in society requires additional knowledge and skill as the routes to empowerment for older people are somewhat different.

This aspect is emphasized because of the widespread acceptance of the belief, and one shared by many older people who have become habituated to it, that older people should gradually disengage themselves from wider society. A related view, often offered as a justification for withholding some benefit or not involving them in some decision is that they have had a 'good innings', a 'fair crack of the whip'. These seemingly kindly and innocuous statements conceal unexamined moral positions which militate against the wellbeing of older people and assign them to a position which would be considered unacceptable for younger people still operating in or available for the labour market. Thus certainly one aspect of gerontological education is what I call 'defensive' or gerontological 'apologetics'. It would be concerned with seeking the philosophical and empirical justification for its being available and worthy of receiving some form of public policy recognition and official support. It would encourage the recognition of the ambiguous position, status and experience of older people and argue for the provision of access to the requisite skills to regain equal status as citizens in actuality and not simply as a formality. This involves the acknowledgement that the provision of this kind of education has an important normative force and is concerned equally with combatting social exclusion or social disqualification as providing opportunities for self-fulfilment and active participation in the cultural life of the community.

Although the emphasis of this discussion has been directed towards the needs of older people an important aspect of gerontological education pertains to the training of all professionals, regardless of discipline or domain, who have dealings with them. It is frequently the case that informing their judgements are unexamined constructs or models about the nature of ageing and the place of older people in society.

It can be argued that gerontological education is a public good with a comparable moral status to that of health care and it is equally necessary both for promoting individual opportunity and a sense of public wellbeing. However, the existence of inequalities in society creates substantial barriers to its acquisition without some form of public support. In consequence it could be argued that public policy should ensure that in one way or another it should be available.

Although not concerned specifically with gerontological education the Kennedy Report: Learning Works, Widening Participation in Further Education offers a normative basis for its justification:

Education has always been a source of vitality and the more people we can include in the community of learning, the greater the benefits to us all. The very process involves interaction between people; it is the means by which the values and wisdom of a society are shared and transmitted across the generations. Education strengthens the ties which bind people. It takes the fear out of difference and encourages tolerance. It helps people to see what makes the world tick and the ways in which they individually and together, can make a difference. It is the likeliest means of creating a modern well-skilled work force, reducing levels of crime and creating participating citizens (Kennedy, 1997: p.6).

Using this statement as a summary of widely accepted recent opinion, it is possible to extrapolate themes which are of particular relevance for the content of gerontological education. These would include the following: helping to understand the changing and diverse inter-generational value systems; stimulating inter-generational tolerance; identifying and combatting the processes which may lead to social exclusion and social disqualification; providing opportunities for developing or revising skills useful for political, social and community action; and exploring the dynamics of becoming old in a changing society. These are in addition to a fair access to facilities for the renewal or acquisition of vocational skills and involvement in the resources of liberal education. The list, by no means exhaustive, is used to demonstrate that the educational values which are identified as being crucial for younger generations are equally of relevance to the experience of older generations, who can reasonable stake a claim for overt recognition and inclusion in public debate.

It can, and has been, argued that the ageing of society presents no special problem for distributive or social justice and accordingly can be contained within this rubric without difficulty. Central to this view is that any inequality in the distribution of fundamental goods and services must not be based upon considerations which are regarded as morally irrelevant. Thus in the distribution of social goods such as health care, educational opportunity, civil liberties, individual traits or the characteristics of individuals such as race, religion, sex and age are regarded as morally irrelevant. In actual distributive contexts, for example, when awarding scholarships, in employment situations or receiving welfare benefits only morally relevant facts appropriate to the situation can be applied. So distributive justice operates both on a category as well as an individual basis. To deny employment to someone wholly competent simply on the grounds of age, or refusing to employ all people above a certain age, regardless of competence, is to apply morally irrelevant criteria. I want to argue that restricting access to older people violates an important principle of distributive justice in the same way as allocating any public good solely on the basis of age and ignoring the appropriate morally relevant criteria. Thus any claim for the incorporation of educational gerontology and gerontological education in public policy must be able to demonstrate that the relevant moral criteria exist.

To justify any claim within a context of social justice two dimensions have to be considered. The first concerns the establishment of the claim; the second, its implementation. Simply for purposes of exposition I stipulate the first as the 'constitutive dimension' and the second the 'distributive dimension'.

The constitutive dimension is concerned with establishing a valid claim for whatever is under consideration to be incorporated into the framework of public policy. The distributive dimension is concerned with the conditions informing its availability and which individuals or groups are entitled to benefit. Thus a 'constitutive' claim may be established but if resources are limited, distributive difficulties may arise because all those with legitimate claims cannot be satisfied and there may have to be a further set of criteria for selecting specific cases as not everyone may be able to be benefit, certainly not in the short run whatever may be the case in the longer term. This is a form of resource allocation or priority setting. This latter element will not be examined as it requires a review of appropriate criteria which are not immediately relevant to the establishment of the general case for gerontological education based upon stronger criteria than beneficence or pragmatism which seems to be the case at present, though neither should be disregarded as having no contribution to make.

The case for gerontological education is located within the context of a modern democratic state with liberal aspirations, no matter how flawed, which has to recognize and acknowledge that there are different legitimate systems of value, some cognate and other distinctively separate. Any agreement reached will need to satisfy or at least not draw the antagonism of any of the several value systems. This means abandoning any idea of a single comprehensive ethical system which has overarching authority and from which principles and practice are derived. Thus justification must not be repugnant to either religious or secular value systems and be able to attract support from each. This inevitably means that ethical doctrines claiming a comprehensive or exclusive nature will not be available to determine claims of social justice. Claims based, for example, upon either variants of utilitarism (using some single principle as an appropriate determinant, such as welfare or preference satisfaction) or deontological theories (using concepts such as duty and obligation) which cannot attract consensual support will be discounted. This approach involves recognising and acknowledging diversity as legitimate in a liberal society and that any consensus must encompass it. Most traditional notions of social justice have comprised theories which have failed to recognise this diversity just as it is only until comparatively recently that the notion of processual social justice has been articulated with its concern for future generations as well as existing ones.

Rawls uses the term 'overlapping consensus' (Rawls, 1996) to describe this particular kind of consensus so that claims pursued under the head of social justice must be able to draw support from it. Practical ethical decisions have to take place in society where a range of considerations both ethical and non-ethical have to be balanced along with the possibility of implementing them in an attempt to achieve an acceptable outcome which is seen in some sense as being fair.

Given the nature of the overlapping consensus, which principles or rights become relevant to the resolution of practical moral dilemmas in the public arena and would attract widespread support? Assuming a liberal democracy, which can be regarded as an attempt to provide a political and social system supporting a high degree of cooperation, reciprocity and tolerance, three rights can be identified as of especial relevance. One underpins every liberal democracy and that is the right of individuals to be treated as equals, which involves being treated with the same concern and respect as others. This has to be distinguished from and is lexically prior to the notion of equal treatment (Dworkin, 1977: p.227). The other two, closely related to this fundamental right, are: (I) equality of opportunity and (ii) the notion of citizenship with its associated rights and duties, and the expectation that the state will honour its obligations to its citizens.

These three rights have been written about extensively and hence no attempt will be made to establish their validity. Rather they will be stipulated and accordingly be used to support the claims made for the provision by public policy for access to educational gerontology. The core of the claim is that access will provide an instrument for the empowerment of older people and perhaps inhibit, or at least challenge those current attitudes, beliefs and policies which tend to disadvantage them.

Attitudinal and political obstacles

As an illustration of the kind of obstacles which may be encountered in the search for the removal of discriminatory practices two areas of particular relevance will be explored: one concerns attitudinal and cognitive explanations for the so-called legitimacy of adverse discrimination; the other relates to the denuding of the political status of older people by denying issues germane to their welfare from entering the political arena.

Educational gerontology has as one element the task to combatting any misinformation about older people which supports adverse discrimination. As this activity constitutes an important part of the supporting case it is important to account for the persistence of adverse discriminatory practices and beliefs. It is certain that a degree of sheer prejudice exists but that only affects a small proportion of those supporting such practices. The majority tend to argue that their attitudes and beliefs about older people have rational foundations. If they are mistaken, how do they obtain their beliefs? Extending the perceptive discussion in Levine (Levine, 1988, chap.16) the term 'cognitive error' is introduced to account for at least some of the reasons for holding age-discriminatory beliefs.

Cognitive error theory draws attention to the common practice of what has been classified as 'satisfying', that is the ready acceptance by individuals or groups of partial explanations for the existence of particular social phenomena. As the partial explanation seems to offer an adequate response for immediate purposes to question it would involve delay and possibly further investigation. This practice is a widespread phenomenon of both private and public discussion and intrudes into official rhetoric and documentation. In consequence it becomes easy for inadequate explanations or beliefs to achieve a spurious validity.

This phenomenon has particular relevance in regards to beliefs about and attitudes towards older people. When making judgements people tend to draw upon pre-existing beliefs, theories, attitudes and values as a method of making sense of their life-worlds. In part this involves the acceptance of stereotypes which are culturally and socially transmitted and which become part of their conceptual universe. They are readily adopted because of their wide acceptance and this fact is frequently cited as an important justification for their validity. Having adopted them, there can be a biased assimilation of evidence, that is evidence which collects examples of behaviour which supports the adopted stereotypes and discounts any which runs counter to them. These stereotypes along with generalisations, that is the ascription to a person of the characteristics of a group without any form of individualised assessment, are taken to constitute factually based judgements. People holding them are in principle acting rationally but on the basis of incorrect or misleading information. Where they are plainly false or misleading it is part of the task of educational gerontology to counter them. This is not a trivial activity for disparaging stereotypes of older people widely persists, not least among older people themselves who have been seduced by their spurious validity. To counter them is part of a programme of restoring the status of older people.

Lukes in a perceptive study of political power (Lukes, 1982) suggests a paradigm of power which contributes to an understanding of the modest appearance of issues relating to the status of older people, discriminatory practices and their relative absence from participation in the political process. This is of particularly relevance to the United Kingdom.

It is not possible to deal with all the ramifications that this paradigm has for older people but, briefly, in the discussion of power the emphasis has usually been placed upon the effectiveness groups or individuals have in influencing the outcomes of political decisions. Indeed, it is argued that older people in the UK are not sufficiently mobilized as a group and are therefore too weak to have any serious impact upon political decision making. What Lukes does in this paradigm is to demonstrate that real political power can be exercised by preventing potential issues from even entering the political arena. So effective may be the exercise of this kind of power that the potential issues may never materialize or be articulated. As Lukes writes:

> ... is not the supreme and most insidious exercise of power to prevent people, to whatever degree, from having grievances by shaping their perceptions, cognitions and preferences in such a way that they accept their role in the existing order of things, either because they see it as natural and unchangeable, or because they value it as divinely ordained and beneficial. To assume that the absence of grievance equals genuine consensus is simply to rule out the possibility of false or manipulated consensus by definitional fiat (Lukes, 1982: p.24).

There is evidence that the legitimate interests of older people frequently have been and are frustrated before they enter the political process and the history of attempts to eradicate discriminatory employment practices may be cited in support of this claim. It would be part of the function of an educational gerontology to help in the articulation and presentation in the public domain of appropriate issues and concerns.

The two previous sections are illustrative of some of the difficulties older people face when endeavouring to express their interests, counter inappropriate generalisations and stereotypes or identifying those barriers which inhibit the placement of their concerns in the public and political arenas. The unintended consequences of cognitive error and the non-recognition of relevant issues constitutes a significant violation of their rights.

Earlier it was argued that three rights were important for older people: the right to treatment as equals, equality of opportunity and the rights associated with citizenship. It may be asserted that these can be best achieved through the normal political processes but I hope the brief illustrative discussion of cognitive error and the possibility of issues being prevented from entering the political domain by interests inimical to those of older people throws doubt on the strength of this claim. For the political process to respond adequately it would require significant changes in both public and private perceptions of the place of older people in contemporary society. Such changes only occur when the prevailing attitudes and belief are challenged and modified. That there is a widespread failure to recognize the rights of older people to treatment as equals is supported by compelling evidence from a range of sources. Equality of opportunity is denied when access to employment or public office is blocked simply by reference to chronological age without evaluating other competences. And the rights of citizens to political participation are frequently denied to older people. Where age alone is used as the sole criterion it invariably involves a violation of fundamental rights.

Educational gerontology cannot be itself solve these problems; it could well be argued that this is not its role. But it does offer an opportunity for older people to regain and assert those rights which have been denuded over time. In seeking to combat unethical discriminatory practices which find justification because of the persistence of suspect evidence it is helping older people to regain their status as equal citizens.

The ethical basis for the claim, similar to and no less important than that associated with racism and sex discrimination, is almost self-evident given a liberal democracy with such a large proportion of the population exposed to these disadvantages. Educational gerontology may not be the only way of helping older people challenge the violations of their rights and reclaiming their status in society but it is the only real tool currently on offer, whatever may happen in the future. Attempts are made by many organisations to address specific problems which beset many older people as, for example, inadequate pensions, poor access to health care, inconvenient housing, but educational gerontology not only includes these matter but offers a comprehensive approach to old age in contemporary society. Access to it will provide a firm basis from which older people can begin to reclaim their dignity and identity. The campaigns to eradicate racism and sex discrimination are based upon ethical considerations comparable to those articulated above and educational gerontology like them is no less worthy of public support.

6 Critical educational gerontology and the imperative to empower

Sandra Cusack

Introduction

'Empowerment' is the unifying concept that brings together, either implicitly or explicitly, diverse approaches within the emerging paradigm of Critical Gerontology, which is, above all, concerned with the 'emancipation of older people from all forms of domination' and 'with identifying possibilities for emancipatory social change, including positive ideals for the last stage of life'. (Moody, 1993, p. xv). As critical gerontologists Minkler (1996) and Phillipson (1994) have suggested, it is through the empowerment of older people that critical gerontology can make its most important contributions to the field of ageing. In a world that is ageing, in Dychtwald's (1997) terms, with the force of a Japanese tidal wave, a new world view of old age is imperative. Critical educational gerontology provides the method and the means for realizing the possibilities and transforming individuals and societies.

The major task is one of liberating people *of all ages* from a view of old age as an expensive, expansive wasteland and older people as useless burdens on society. The new longevity - the 30 years added to the average life span in the last 100 years - demands that we embrace 'old age' as the most significant human achievement of the 20th Century. This new perspective on the extended life span invites us to take bold steps to develop the human potential for growth and productivity to the end of life, whether that comes at age 65 or 110. The human potentials movement of the 1960s takes on greater significance and a certain urgency in the new *millenium of older people*, with new possibilities and imperatives for self-actualization in the later years. A formidable task, and one that gives the education of older adults a critical and central role.

Older Adult Education is one of five areas of expertise at the Gerontology Research Centre, Simon Fraser University. During the past decade, we have developed a programme of research and teaching that focuses on developing seniors as community leaders and service-providers. Our approach to research and programme development is supported by a philosophy of 'research as emancipatory education'; that is to say, the conduct of research is explicitly designed to liberate people from old attitudes and assumptions about ageing and what it means to be old, and to open them up to new possibilities. Similarly, our approach to teaching third-age adults (aged 50 to 90+) focuses on the empowerment of individuals, groups, and organizations through the application of specific principles and techniques that enable people to make personal change and to work together toward common goals.

Consistent with Battersby's (1987) notion of gerogogy, our approach to teaching is informed by critical theory and the liberation theology of Paulo Freire. We agree with Battersby and others that teaching *older* adults is qualitatively different from teaching adults, because the social circumstances and developmental tasks of third-age persons in today's world is unique. While educational gerontologists may not agree that old people are generally oppressed and disenfranchised, we *can* all agree that old age is something we neither aspire to nor look forward to. Has anyone of 35 years, or 40, or even 50, said they can't wait to be 65? Yet many people who are 65 today say it is the 'best time of their lives'. We know one woman of 80 who claims she is healthier and happier than she was at 65. Do we believe her? Or do we think she must be 'losing it'? We used to say 'life begins at 40', now many people say 'life begins at 50'. In fact, one of the latest euphemisms is 'Don't trust anyone *under* 50'.

What is unique about teaching people aged 50+ that distinguishes older adult education from adult education generally conceived? Why is older adult education *more* than adult education targeting a particular client group? From a social constructivist perspective, the answer is obvious. Society has constructed a negative image of ageing and old people - we assume that ageing is characterized by inevitable decline in mental faculties, failing health, physical and emotional loss, and those who live to a 'ripe old age' are the 'survivors'. We must, therefore, deconstruct and reconstruct our images of ageing and older people, and reconstruction is particularly crucial for people aged 50+ because they have grown up and are growing old with limiting beliefs and assumptions developed over a lifetime that are entrenched and *must* be eradicated. The empowerment, i.e., liberation and transformation, of older people through education must be intentional and explicit.

The purpose of this chapter is (1) to locate the approach, critical *educational* gerontology within critical gerontology; (2) to operationalize the concept of 'empowerment' in two specific subject/content areas: leadership training and mental fitness; (3) through the reflective analysis of practice, as suggested by

Battersby (1993), to identify techniques designed to empower; and (4) to provide evidence in narrative form that exemplifies what it means and what it feels like to be empowered.

Critical gerontology and the educational imperative

A number of perspectives have emerged during the past 20 years that provoke critical examination of the way in which academic gerontology has defined old age as a problem and old people as a burden. Minkler (1996) conceptualizes critical gerontology as evolving along two paths. The first, reflected in the political economy of ageing, is embodied in the works of scholars such Estes, Phillipson, Walker, and Minkler. This perspective provides a framework within which to understand old age as a problem, characterized by inequalities in the distribution of power, income and property.

The second approach, the humanistic, is exemplified in the works of scholars such as Achenbaum, Cole, and Moody. Moody (1988) and others are critical of the technical and instrumental orientation of academic gerontology that focuses on managing ageing bodies with increasing efficiency and no consideration for the political context or the meaning and significance of life. A humanistic orientation seeks to encompass body, mind, and spirit, and to give voice to the meaning of growing old. Both humanistic and political economy streams shed light on the extent to which older people are 'disempowered' whether through structural constraints or lack of a sense of meaning and purpose.

In her review of public policy and the condition of older adults, Estes (1993) concluded that empowerment to the fullest extent possible must be the goal of public policy and scholars must give as much research attention to questions of empowerment and equity as to those of cost and efficiency. The same year, *Ageing International* devoted an entire volume to the topic of empowerment, and the empowerment of senior citizens was identified as a global priority (Thurz, et al., 1993). The imperative to empower has implications for every area of practice in working with older people, and must be considered within the various contexts and cultures.

Since the early 1980s, practical applications of empowerment have been somewhat haphazard. In the context of social work practice, Cox and Parsons (1994) outline an empowerment-oriented approach. In the context of long-term care, Brink (1993) and Hofland (1994) discuss changes in the nursing home environment that empower residents (e.g., increasing personal choice). Roberto et al. (1994) and Tebb (1995) focus on empowering caregivers. Others (NB., Wallerstein and Bernstein, 1988; Wallerstein, 1992; Minkler, 1985; Ramji, 1995) have refined and adapted Paulo Freire's concept of empowerment as part of the health promotion movement.

Efforts to empower have suffered somewhat from the misuse and abuse of the term, and notably, its use as rhetoric to support programmes that pay lip service to the intention, yet fail to operationalize the construct within specific contexts or document outcomes. Clarke (1987) refers to empowerment as the 'buzzword' of the 1980s and questions whether empowerment in the context of medicine serves the best interests of older adults. While, at a conceptual level, the empowerment of seniors has been thoughtfully and critically explored and debated by critical gerontologists around the world, practice has suffered in the absence of practical, reasoned, and deliberate application within particular contexts and the absence of evaluations that document the desired individual and social change. Those who do it, don't talk about it and don't analyze it: those who experience it, rarely use the word, empowerment. A major barrier has been a lack of appreciation for the societal value of both age-segregated and age-integrated education for older adults and hence a lack of funding for the research and development of educational programmes designed to empower.

This chapter offers a conceptual analysis of empowerment in the context of two specific subject areas of later life teaching and learning: leadership and mental fitness. The purpose of the analysis is to provide a framework for the research and development of educational programmes and services that truly empower - in other words, they contribute to both individual and societal transformation. Within such a framework, programmes and services designed to empower can and must address the following questions:

- What is it that is 'disempowering' to seniors in this context?
- Who has the power (individuals, agencies)?
- What do we mean by 'empowerment'?
- What are people being 'empowered' to do?
- How are people being empowered? Process, techniques, principles?
- How do we know it's working? What evidence do we have of individual and collective empowerment?

In 1997, a symposium was convened at the World Congress on Gerontology in Australia entitled, *Empowering Senior Citizens around the World through Education.* Contexts for empowerment were (1) a seniors' wellness programme at a health centre in Australia (Hatton, 1997); (2) a seniors' education programme at a university in Chile (Kornfeld, 1997); (3) an intergenerational health promotion programme in Africa (Ramji, 1997) and (4) an advocacy project in 15 European countries (Webster, 1997). While empowering older people was the specific intention of service-providers in every instance, the concept was neither operationalized nor discussed in any of the programmes, although it was the focus for academic discussion at the conference.

64

During the question period, Peter Laslett, father of the Third-age Education movement in Great Britain, asked, 'Why not just let older people do it themselves? Why do they need to be 'empowered''? The simple answer is because most senior leaders and teachers have little awareness of the extent to which the majority of their peers are 'disempowered' nor do they have the skill or the political will to empower them. The complete answer is more complex, and in many ways, this chapter represents a reasoned response to Laslett's question.

Older adults who provide educational leadership for their peers rarely have an appreciation for the life-experiences of the vast majority of older people who have not enjoyed the advantages of higher education and whose options in life and creative expression have always been and continue to be limited. Furthermore, our research in seniors centres in Canada, suggests that traditional leaders typically exercise their own power and authority at the expense of others. Rarely do they have either the sensitivity or the skill required to share the power and the leadership with others (Cusack, 1998).

Older adults who serve as teachers (e.g. in U3A in the UK and learning-in -retirement programmes in America) may have a style of teaching that is traditional, that worked for them but not for the majority of people aged 50+ who were never well-served by education at any time in their lives. Furthermore, facilitating learning for older adults is a skill that few people *of any age* have fully developed, and empowering older people is essentially an educational process - it is, as Battersby (1993) suggests, what happens in the discourse and dialogue between two people who are both learning and teaching.

Empowerment means reframing old notions of 'power over' to embrace 'power to' and 'power with' approaches, and enabling seniors to play a greater role in setting the community-based research agenda, and shaping the policies and programmes that affect them. With regard to ageing research, applying an empowerment perspective requires that researchers rethink ways in which they formulate research questions, and gather data, and even some of the concepts and assumptions upon which research is based. Those for whom services are designed, older people themselves, must be engaged as equal partners in the conduct of research, in defining essential concepts and the language of common discourse, and framing programmes designed to address not just their needs, but also their aspirations. A research project with the empowerment of individuals and groups as a primary objective engages older people themselves in every aspect of an enquiry grounded in a philosophy of research as emancipatory education (Cusack and Thompson, 1999, in prep.).

While the body of literature on empowerment grows, there is little theory to guide professionals working with older people in transferring greater legitimate responsibility for decision-making to seniors and enabling them to assume more effective leadership roles in the delivery of programmes and services to their peers. In the context of seniors' recreation centres, many have suggested (e.g. Ross,

1991), that recreation professionals simply step aside and let seniors run things themselves. However, such an approach is naive and fails to recognize the organizational structure and political context within which seniors and professionals typically work together.

Empowering seniors as leaders

Leadership training cannot be considered apart from the organizational culture in which it is imbedded. When a programme is designed that reflects a deep understanding of the culture, the required training can then be offered that will increase the understanding of the leader-student, enhance his or her leadership skills, and improve the quality of leadership. To be highly successful, people need more than just a training programme. They need and deserve the kind of expert training that is intentionally and explicitly empowering.

What is 'disempowering' to seniors in the context of seniors organizations? Seniors are often disempowered by traditional leaders - seniors leaders and/or staff who are authoritarian in their approach. In some organizations, the men are 'in charge' and sexist language and assumptions rob women of their power, as was the case in Centennial Centre, a seniors' centre in western Canada (Cusack and Thompson, 1998, in prep.). But most disempowering and destructive are the general attitudes and assumptions about leadership and about inevitable decline with age.

Who has the power? To some extent, every organization is unique in its structural-functionalist distribution of power, and who has the 'real' power is rarely obvious. In seniors' organizations, a style of traditional leadership gives power to managers, directors, and to the board. In some cases, professionals may have all the power and senior leaders may have little legitimate power to make decisions, particularly where money is power and programmes are subsidized (Cusack, 1998).

What do we mean by 'empowerment'? We mean sharing responsibility and enabling seniors to take a more active role in decision-making processes and in delivering services to their peers. Empowerment means developing leadership skill, extending legitimate authority and responsibility, and giving people the recognition, support, and encouragement they need to be successful.

What are people being 'empowered' to do? In many organizations today, senior volunteers are being empowered to do work that was formerly done by staff. Many who do not see themselves as leaders and have no confidence in their

66

potential as leaders are being called upon to share the workload in delivering programmes and services to their peers.

How are they being empowered? They are being empowered by sensitive, empowering professional leaders who give them what they need to become successful leaders, including the best education and training that is available.

What kind of education empowers seniors? The teacher/facilitator who intends to empower others does not give up authority and responsibility, but actively works to transfer responsibility for learning to students. Empowering pedagogy (or andragogy) involves a shift in power as domination to power as creative energy. A view of power as creative energy requires that strategies be developed to counteract unequal power relationships and to move the dynamics toward equality of power.

Empowering pedagogy involves a continuous process of dialogue and negotiation between facilitator and learner with the emphasis on balancing individual and group training needs. Confidence in one's leadership skills and abilities does not occur as a result of injections of topics x, y, and z, but develops through continuous discussion, practice, feedback, reflection, and renegotiation with the focus on topics that relate to the tasks involved in leadership. The essence of andragogy is classroom discussion and the facilitator must be highly skilled, able to incorporate strategies for facilitating new learning and critical thinking.

Seniors who participated in a leadership training programme were clear that a skilled facilitator was essential to any educational programme. They said that the teacher/facilitator must be one who

- understands that the participants are the experts, and the teacher is the guide;
- is a good listener, has a lot of patience, and good control of the more vocal ones in a group;
- takes a participatory approach, sets ground rules, deals with feelings, and ensures that everyone can see and hear;
- ensures that everyone has an opportunity to engage in discussion, the shy and quiet ones may need extra encouragement;
- gets group feedback and adapts each session accordingly;
- respects the contribution that seniors have to give and the wisdom they have accumulated over the years;
- challenges and stimulates thinking in order to change attitudes that block new insights;
- believes in each person's potential and the possibility for new growth;
- uses humour effectively;

67

- never underestimate what seniors have to offer; there is no limit to what they know and what they can do.

The success of any leadership training programme may rest on whether someone with the essential skills can be engaged to facilitate the training. And as part of the training programme, the facilitator must help people to understand and deal with issues of power and conflict, and to function as empowering leaders.

What does it mean 'to be empowered' in the context of a leadership training programme?

Those who are empowered become visibly more energetic and vital. Empowerment is expressed as a psychological process that makes people feel good. It also leads to individual and collective action that benefits the whole community. This is how people in a leadership project described what they gained from a leadership training programme (Cusack and Thompson, 1995):

My preconceived ideas of retirement kept getting in my way of actively participating in various projects of interest to me. This programme has removed these inhibitions, and given me a real kick start to once again enjoy the satisfaction of involvement. That feeling of being empowered is great. This programme has given full meaning to the word. E - enthusiastic, M - motivated, P - powerful, O- optimistic, W-wise, E-energetic, R-revitalized (Doris Bloomfield, participant, *Leadership for the 90s' Project*).

I was able to modify my leadership style from an authoritarian to a shared - servant leadership approach. I have increased confidence in assuming roles and responsibilities. I have improved my communication and observation skills with individuals and groups. I have enhanced my organizational problem-solving skills which were always fairly strong I have increased knowledge of group dynamics and interaction resulting in improved facilitation skills. I have more awareness of the needs of seniors and I am in a better position to help other seniors meet their needs. I have gained a deeper appreciate of the value of humour in working and interacting with people, and I have acquired some tools that I can use in facilitating workshops (Rollie Hennessey, participant, *Leadership for the 90s' Project*).

The whole community benefits when we take our new leadership skills into groups outside our centre. More new volunteers come forward as they gain confidence. With more volunteers, the workload is shared. Furthermore, new volunteers bring new ideas and energy to the community, often becoming leaders themselves and developing new programmes that are of benefit to the community (Jerrine Jago, participant, *Leadership for the 90's Project*).

A member of the class described both individual and group transformation and offered her personal reflections on how it was achieved:

A group of retirees have now completed the first phase of a leadership development project designed to prepare them to facilitate the emergence of a new approach to leadership in our seniors' centre. As a member of the group, I have observed the transformation of a noncohesive collection of individuals (aged 50 to 75) with diverse histories into a cohesive and homogeneous, tolerant, confident, assertive, and productive group. How did we manage this metamorphosis in such a short time?

We started by absorbing the principles of Shared-Servant Leadership, an approach promoted in the training manual, *Flying High: A Guide to Shared Leadership in Retirement*. We were then engaged in identifying our individual training needs, while encouraging and supporting each other to develop their individual potential and to share the leadership. Participants were given equal opportunity to speak and to share their points of view, as well as to share their skills and talents. The respect given to each person's views and experience enabled them to recognize and share their strengths.

The first step in developing self-confident leaders was building confidence by motivating, encouraging and supporting each member' efforts. For example, participants were asked to introduce another member of the group, and introductions were followed by positive feedback for their efforts. While practicing and developing skills in communicating our ideas in an interesting way, we all developed a feeling of acceptance by the group, despite our personal limitations. Positive feedback from the group helped people to cope with frustrations and nervousness, and promoted feelings of strength and confidence.

Opportunities to build self-confidence and develop speaking skills were presented at each session. For example, participants were given opportunities to introduce the session, share a joke or poem with the group, and report on any events or books relating to shared leadership. Each session was designed to heighten our sense of self-worth, while developing listening and communication skills by using appropriate assertive and supportive language as well as defining, adjusting, assessing, and restructuring our personal development goals.

During the first phase of the programme, I have myself gone through a profound change. I began the course somewhat reluctantly with a negative attitude towards groups based on a lifetime of experience with autocratic group leadership that suppressed individuality and creativity. This group has been a new experience for me. I have learned to communicate more effectively and with more sensitivity to the needs of others in the group. I have come to enjoy sharing ideas in a group and I have a new feeling of acceptance and freedom to express myself (Sedlak, 1995).

These observations provide dramatic evidence of individual liberation and transformation. People gained the freedom to express themselves; they gained confidence in their capacity for leadership, and moved to a higher level of contribution, while supporting and encouraging each other to create a united team.

Empowering seniors in a mental fitness class

In the context of a mental fitness course, personal empowerment is central to the educational experience; and critical thinking is both a key component of mental fitness and a teaching technique that is used throughout the programme.

What is it that is 'disempowering' to seniors? Most disempowering and disabling are the many negative beliefs and assumptions that people hold about ageing and older people. The most important and most destructive is the general belief that ageing means inevitable decline in mental abilities and the fear that older people have about losing their mental faculties.

Who has the power (individuals, agencies)? In an ageist society, particularly in the present high-tech knowledge economy, younger people and especially those who are skilled with communications technology have a greater share of the power. In a classroom, a skilled facilitator has the power - the skill and the ability to empower participants.

What do we mean by 'empowerment'? In a mental fitness programme, empowering participants means liberating them from limiting beliefs about ageing and their own abilities, working with them to develop their mental fitness skills, and giving people the knowledge, the confidence, and the support they need to continue to learn and develop their mental abilities to the end of life.

What are people being 'empowered' to do? People are being empowered to believe in their own mental abilities and their capacity to create their own futures; and they are challenged, motivated, and encouraged to make healthy lifestyle changes and continue to develop their mental fitness. They are also empowered to value all older persons and the contribution they can make to society.

How are people being empowered?

A mental fitness course uses many of the tools and techniques that empower learners in any adult education. However, the most important technique that is modelled and developed is that of critical thinking, a powerful method for challenging the negative assumptions people have about ageing, and replacing them with alternate, more positive beliefs and assumptions. In academic circles, critical thinking is synonymous with logical analysis -the opposite of creative or divergent thinking. In common everyday use, critical thinking may have a negative connotation - to be critical is to be negative and distrusting. Brookfield (1989) in his book, *Developing Critical Thinkers*, lays out a method of 'critical thinking' that is designed to challenge the beliefs and assumptions we hold that may be either erroneous or no longer useful. First, he provides the following insights into assumptions and how we acquire them:

> Assumptions are the seemingly self-evident rules about reality that we use to help us seek explanations, make judgments, or decide on various actions. They are the unquestioned givens that, to us, have the status of self-evident truths. People cannot reach adulthood without bringing with them frameworks of understanding and sets of assumptions that undergird their decisions, judgments, and actions. These assumptions influence how we understand cause-and-effect relationships (for example, seeing crime as the result of poverty as opposed to laziness). They inform our criteria regarding what is good behaviour in others (for example, showing concern for others' misfortunes, ignoring conventional mores, ruthlessly pursuing one's self-interest). Assumptions help construct our understanding of what we judge to be 'human nature' . . . (and) they shape how we view the political world (p. 44).

Critical thinking is a step-by-step process for getting rid of the assumptions that underlie our belief systems and habitual ways of thinking and acting. It involves so much more than the skills of logical analysis taught in so many academic courses on critical thinking. It means calling into question the assumptions underlying our customary, habitual ways of thinking and acting and then being ready to think and act differently on the basis of this critical questioning.

What is critical thinking? According to Brookfield, critical thinking is a productive and positive activity, a process and not an outcome; and it is both

71

emotive and rational. Manifestations of critical thinking vary according to the contexts in which it occurs. In the context of seniors mental fitness programmes it means identifying and erasing limiting beliefs about the inevitably decline of mental abilities. It can be triggered by both positive and negative events, though it is typically triggered by negative limiting language. Negative attitudes are associated with negative emotions such as anger and depression. The components of critical thinking are challenging assumptions; recognizing the importance of context; imagining and exploring alternative beliefs; and maintaining an attitude of reflective scepticism.

The seven steps to critical thinking in the context of mental fitness are as follows:

1 Identify a negative, limiting statements/language.

2 Identify limiting belief(s) and assumptions that underly the statement and the language.

3 Challenge the validity of that limiting belief.

4 Explore alternative more optimistic and positive beliefs.

5 Create an argument within yourself to replace the old belief with a new one.

6 Create a new statement using the language of possibility.

7 Be aware!

Critical thinking skills were used effectively in the Mental Fitness Pilot Progams (Cusack and Thompson, 1998a) as a technique to challenge the assumptions that people have about ageing that limit their options for a healthy old age, and changing negative beliefs to positive beliefs about the limitless possibilities for growth and development in later life.

How do we know it's working? What is the evidence for empowerment?

Evidence that people are using their critical thinking skills and feeling a sense of liberation and transformation comes from the participant observation records of the programme. The voices of participants provide the most compelling evidence that the programme is working, for example, the said things like ...

I used to believe that old age meant gradual decline in body and mind, and that I had to learn to accept my limitations in an uncomplaining way and look for the joy in nature and those things that endure. Now I believe that no matter what the future holds, there will be new goals and activities to challenge my mind and abilities (Eunice Ellis, participant, *Mental Fitness Pilot Programme*).

I have a newfound energy that is enabling me to think more clearly. I am doing things I never thought I could because of this excitement I have. I am striving for things I never thought I could achieve. Perhaps it was the limiting beliefs that held me back (Dot Josey, Participant, *Mental Fitness Pilot Programme*).

Barbara Guttmann-Gee was a participant in the most recent programme (Cusack and Thompson, 1998b). Her personal story describes how she benefited personally and what she was able to achieve. Her story is particularly important, because the programme was initially designed for people who were not comfortable taking educational classes, but were concerned about keeping their minds sharp. Barbara's story tells us that the programme works for everyone, regardless of their level of education.

Barbara Guttmann-Gee is a woman 84 years of age who grew up in England and qualified for Oxford University at the age of 16. However, the Depression and the War intervened and education had to be postponed. She married and emigrated to Canada where she worked in secretarial jobs most of her life. When she retired, she enrolled in the Open Learning Institute and received a B.A. in her 70s, then an M.A. in Women's Studies from Simon Fraser University at 81.

Physically, she fits the stereotype of the 'sweet little old lady' - but like all stereotypes, it fails to convey the richness of her experience, the razor-sharpness of her mind, and the ability to speak her mind eloquently when the opportunity arises and the spirit moves her. Before she undertook a course of university studies, Barbara fully expected that her mental faculties would diminish with age. Research for a Master's degree together with personal experience as a student changed her belief in the inevitable decline of mental abilities. Her mental ability continues to improve, because she has a desire to be happy and to keep her mind active.

In the Spring of 1998, without a course at the university, she felt that she was getting both mentally and physically lazy, and needed something to get her back on track, so she enrolled in a Mental Fitness programme at the seniors' centre. She wanted to gain confidence and new knowledge that would fuel her keen interest in destroying the myth that mental faculties decline with age. 'For the rest of my life, I shall be fighting for older people, so that with mental and physical fitness they can hold their heads up. We have so much that is on the shelf'.

A key component of the programme involves setting and achieving personal mental fitness goals. Barbara's personal mental fitness goal was to get more confidence and knowledge to support her mission in life, which is to foster education for older people. As part of her goal, she spoke to a group of students at the university who were studying how to teach older people. She spoke about her experiences as a senior student, and was highly critical of the quality of instruction at the university. She gave students tips to improve instruction for their senior learners, and impressed them with her spirit of adventure.

On the final day of the Mental Fitness class, participants are asked to provide an update on their goals and achievements. Barbara reported that she had been interviewed on television.

> Last week I was a guest on a TV show entitled *Generations*. I was asked to speak about the importance of learning, and why I was driven to go back to school and get a BA and then an MA. I spoke about the Mental Fitness programme and about new research that suggests the brain doesn't deteriorate with age. When you get older, there can be a lot of 'clutter in the attic', but you just have to get rid of it. If you let your muscles go, they deteriorate and the same is true for the brain. In fact, something vital may go, but the brain can still remain active. If you have a goal, something that drives you on, and you forget your aches and pains. This class has helped me enormously. It got the adrenaline going again, and I was able to make more progress.

An unexpected benefit of the class was a change in attitude toward her peers and the development of new friendships. Raised in Victorian England, Barbara has always proudly managed on her own. For many years, she had pursued her studies independently, and her solitary independent lifestyle put her at serious risk of isolation in later years. She felt she had little in common with people of her own age, and preferred her own company or the company of younger students. In the Mental Fitness class she realized the value of group discussion, marvelled at the achievements of others in the class, and developed a new respect and new social connections with her peers.

With respect to maintaining a high level of mental fitness for the rest of her life, Barbara expressed a particular joy in developing bonds with younger people and seeing herself as intellectually equal.

> Sometimes we are loathe to push ourselves on younger people. I have a surrogate granddaughter and she and her friends (aged 25 to 35) want to know what I think about all kinds of things, and they are fascinated with my stories. Any way that we can find to contribute to others creates health.

Our experience in the research and development of older adult education programmes confirms, time and again, that when older people are given opportunities for personal development (e.g. in the context of leadership training and mental fitness), the benefits go well beyond the group of people taking the course. Participants often seek opportunities for intergenerational learning and exchange of service, and want to make a contribution to society. As Barbara says, education and active engagement in community life are health promoting. Furthermore, all members of the community, regardless of age, gain a better understanding of how important education and learning are throughout life, and they gain greater respect for the mental abilities of older people from their associations with senior leaders who are powerful role models. If we fail to establish 'empowerment' as a central and essentially contested concept within the field of educational gerontology, we jeopardize the most powerful aspect of older adult education - its use as a tool for transforming old age from a period of decline and dependency to one of challenge and productivity.

7 Educational and social gerontology: necessary relationships

The relation between educational gerontology and social gerontology is unclear. It has never been debated in public and this chapter offers some notes for a future agenda.

Educational gerontology in the USA

The origins in the USA of educational gerontology have already been lightly sketched in chapter one. The first person to identify the educational needs of older people was Donahue in *Education for Later Maturity* (1955). Although education for older adults remained the primary focus of the field in the 1950s and 1960s, educational gerontology in the USA came to include both education for older adults and education about ageing.

In 1976, Peterson attempted boldly to define what by then was being called *educational gerontology*, and produced this definition: 'a field of study and practice that has recently developed at the interface of adult education and social gerontology' (Peterson, 1976: p.62). In 1978, Agruso described it as 'the branch of gerontology designed to research hypotheses of the conditions of intellectual development for the elderly ... so that a situation can be established for maximum achievement in each group' (Agruso, 1978: p.4). In the 1978 (first edition) of Sherron and Lumsden's *Introduction to Educational Gerontology*, the editors referred to educational gerontology in a different way as 'a dynamic, fast-growing, new branch of social gerontology' (Sherron and Lumsden, 1978: p.xi).

By the third edition in 1990, the editors were expressing the hope that 'the book will further establish educational gerontology as a legitimate and academically respectable branch of social gerontology' (p.xi). At no stage do these three statements ever appear to have been considered alongside one another, bringing together educational/social gerontology and adult education.

Older Americans were for many decades among the most disadvantaged members of society. As a growing awareness was realised of the quickening pace of demographic ageing and the accompanying social problems that this would inevitably bring, it became apparent that there was a general disinterest in academe in the subject. This moved a handful of scholars during the 1940s, 1950s and 1960s to examine how their own fields of study could contribute to an understanding of the social aspects of ageing. This was particularly true of psychology, sociology, biology, medicine and social work. For this reason, American social gerontology developed as a multi-disciplinary field of study. More and more people, including many educators, gravitated to gerontology, some to contribute to its development, but rather more to exploit its potential. This led scholars like H.R. Johnson to urge that servicing agencies and funding sources should not be allowed to seduce or coerce existing gerontologists into compromising their academic integrity in exchange for money (Johnson, 1980).

As early as 1968, social gerontology had been defined 'as the study of the impact of aging upon individuals and society and the subsequent reactions of individuals and society to aging' (Koller, 1968: p.4). Harris and Cole suggested that 'in the 1950s social gerontology was created as a subfield of gerontology, dealing with the behavioural aspects of ageing and containing other specialities in such disciplines as, economics, political science, anthropology and sociology' (Harris and Cole, 1980: p.6). While Bond et al. In introducing their text on social gerontology wrote:

> The study of ageing is a multidisciplinary enterprise. Each discipline brings its own theoretical perspectives and methods ... They make different assumptions, use concepts in different ways, pose different questions and arrive at different explanations of the ageing process. The perspectives are not right or wrong, simply different (Bond et al., 1993: p.19).

Cole, writing in a different context argues that scientific enquiry cannot replace progress if it regards age merely as a technical problem. 'Old age is an experience to be lived meaningfully' (Cole, 1992: p.237). Moody describes it similarly as 'a lived experience' (Moody, 1988: p.32), which as Phillipson suggests, 'demands a dialogue between the old person, the academic community, practitioners and other relevant groups' (Phillipson, 1998: p.22). Without this, Moody sees the conventional categories that we use as producing 'a shrunken and fragmented view of what this life course might be' (Moody, 1988: p.35).

Reflecting on the genesis of the sociology of ageing in the 1950s, Lynott and Lynott have argued that ageing 'was seen as a process whereby individuals - not social systems, structures of domination or ideologies - hope to alter themselves in some way to deal satisfactorily with their experiences. The problem was not retirement, poverty, ill health and/or social isolation *per se*: these were the conditions [which] were accepted by researchers as the way things were, the facts of elderly life' (Lynott and Lynott, 1996: p.750).

The development of academic gerontology

Against this definitional background the growth of American gerontology has resulted in a flood of publications over the last thirty years. Warnes identified 50,000 titles by 1975 (Warnes, 1989). Multidisciplinary gerontology courses were identified on more than 500 campuses, with professional specialisation taking place in 30 per cent of higher education institutions (Peterson, 1987).

In the UK, development of academic gerontology became increasingly apparent in the 1980s, although at a much slower rate than in the USA. As in America, so in the UK, higher education was very slow to respond. For several decades, British scholars such as Comfort and Medawar in biology and Townsend in applied social studies achieved a considerable scholarly influence. 'British social gerontology in its protracted infancy was most nurtured by those directly involved in the elaboration of social policy and the improvement of social welfare practice' (Warnes, 1989: p.196). Research units began to develop in the late 1970s.

The 1980s also saw the gradual development of academic gerontology in some British universities. In the late 1980s, the first two chairs in social gerontology were created at Keele and London Universities. A few others have followed since. Distinctive contributions to social gerontology have been made by Townsend, Walker and Phillipson in the field of social policy, and by Bromley, Rabitt and Stuart-Hamilton in developmental and cognitive psychology.

The way in which gerontology developed academically in the UK resulted in the British Society of Gerontology in its early years showing scant commitment to third age education, in spite of the launch of the *Journal of Educational gerontology* (now *Education and Ageing*) in 1986. Academic gerontology courses, where they exist, have tended not to include education for older adults in their syllabi, in spite of the considerable contribution made by luminaries such as Laslett and Midwinter to the study of third age education. Further, the relationship between educational and social gerontology has never been the subject of public debate, although Tyler pondered it in a paper some years ago (Tyler, 1991: p.76). This may be the time to define terms.

Definitions of terms used

A. *Social Gerontology* (SG) is concerned with the social aspects of ageing and as such has always been an area of multidisciplinary study.

B. *Educational Gerontology* (EG) is concerned with (1) the education and learning potential of older adults including all relevant aspects and processes.

C. *Gerontological Education* (GE) is concerned with education about the realities of an ageing society; and the training of those who wish to work for and among older people, whether they be professional, para-professional or acting in a voluntary capacity. In general terms this may be described as teaching gerontology. The questions broached at the beginning of this chapter concerned the view that EG is at the interface of SG and adult education and that EG is a 'branch' of SG.

Increasingly in recent years, as has been said, a distinction has been made between educational gerontology (education in the later years) and gerontological education (teaching gerontology). Educational gerontology has thus become a generic term, to cover both EG and GE. In a sense, in the UK, then we have reverted to American practice, although recognising the need for clearer definition, recalling that Lowy regarded GE as being a sub-set of EG (Lowy and O'Connor, 1986: p.12)!

D. *Adult Education* in the UK, while it developed historically from the early Mechanics' Institutes of the 1820s, later in the century we saw the development of 'extra-mural' courses organised by Oxford and Cambridge Universities in different parts of the country. It did not begin to move forward until the 1944 Education Act, where Section 41 of the Act laid it upon local education authorities to be responsible for arranging educational opportunities for those beyond the compulsory school age, 'who are willing and able to profit by the facilities provided for that purpose'. Colleges of Further Education then in theory joined the existing providers of adult education (principally, the Workers' Educational Association and the university extra-mural departments, which after the 1950s grew in number). But this responsibility often seemed to be far from mandatory. Certainly after the Conservative government came to power in 1979, the government was unsympathetic to public expenditure for many years with dire results for British adult education. As a result, apart from the indefatigable work of Peter Jarvis and a few others there cannot be said to exist an actual corpus of British adult educational theory. Remarkably little theoretical work overall appears to have been achieved in the USA either, even though the existence of adult education is well acknowledged by Lowy and O'Connor: 'The lack of a philosophical framework for educational gerontology has been true of all adult education', although they maintain that *Philosophical Foundations of Adult Education* (Elias and Merriam, 1980) is an exception to the rule (Lowy and

O'Connor, 1986: pp.17-27). However, we have previously mentioned, in chapter 2, the contribution made by Knowles, who himself would add Houle, Dewey, Brumer and others (Knowles, 1988).

In the main, while writing in America about adult education, and indeed third age education, has tended to be descriptive or programmatic, but one element that heretofore has been missing has been the absence of any serious study of the effect of the international self-help education movement in relation to third age education. It is essential to address this and Figure 1 allows for this in (3) and (4).

It may be helpful to develop the discussion with a commentary on Figure 1 which is in the form of a matrix to distinguish between the study and practice of educational gerontology and gerontological education. The topics for audience, study and practice listed under the categories of educational gerontology and gerontological education may be developed in this way:

A. Educational Gerontology (learning in the later years).

1. *Instructional Gerontology:* How older people function; including early school leavers from 40-50 years ago and their learning situation; environmental context; educational motivation; the psychology of learning; memory and intelligence; learning aptitude; programme models; teaching method and style; good practice, theory and research.

2. *Senior Adult Education:* Enabling older adults to extend their range of knowledge and skills, through reflecting on their experience; assessment of student needs; training of tutors and facilitators; curriculum development; marketing and delivery; evaluation.

3. *Self-help instructional gerontology:* learning and helping others to learn in a self-help mode; establishing a curriculum and methodology; how to establish standards; access to educational institutions; encountering distrust of formalism; need for independence; consumer sensitivity; developmental potential; relationships in the learning group, especially between facilitator and participant; good practice, theory and research.

4. *Self-help senior adult education:* learning groups; coping skills; peer counselling; self-health care; learning activities; participation and environment; dialogue and problem solving; meeting the needs of the housebound or long-term patients in care homes and hospitals; frail elderly and reminiscence; administration; assistance; travel problems.

81

Figure 1: Categories of Educational Gerontology and Gerontological Education

A. Educational Gerontology (Learning in the Later Years)

	Older People and Adult Educators	Older people: animateurs, adult educators, (in post or retired)
Audience		
Study	1. Instructional Gerontology	3. Self-help Instructional Gerontology
Practice	2. Senior Adult Education	4. Self-help Senior Adult Education

B. Gerontological Education (Teaching Gerontology)

	Older people and the general public	Professionals and para-professionals	Professionals, para-professionals and volunteers
Audience			
Study	5. Social Gerontology and Adult Education		
Practice	6. Advocacy Gerontology	7. Professional Gerontology (professional training)	8. Gerontology Education (in-service and post-qualifying training)

Source: © Glendenning (1990: p.15)

B. Gerontological Education (teaching gerontology)

5. *Social Gerontology:* stereotypes and myths of older people; attitude change; research-based information about the ageing process and aspects of an ageing society; modes of communication with makers of social policy, families, social workers, health visitors, nurses, medical doctors and consultants; critical reflection on the implementation of social action.

and adult education: curriculum development for gerontology and other courses; tutor training; process of learning; good practice, theory and research methodology.

6. *Advocacy gerontology:* consciousness-raising based on accurate information; familiarity with issues such as pensions, benefits, long-term care, housing, assault and abuse; discrimination (both ageist, sexist and racial); over-prescription of drugs; old people as a mainstream resource in society; presenting the case to politicians, social policy makers, medical profession, nurses and social workers, younger people; enabling older people to become citizen advocates.

7. *Professional gerontology:* professional training of skilled tutors and practitioners; curriculum development; criteria for validation; course evaluation; management of services.

8. *Gerontology education:* post-professional and post-qualifying training; curriculum development; in-service training; training of volunteers; updating of management skills; community strategies; role and needs of carers.

Educational gerontology at the interface

In the light of all this, it is worth returning to examine Peterson's view that educational gerontology stands at the interface of adult education and social gerontology and also the view of Sherron and Lumsden that educational gerontology is 'a fast growing branch of social gerontology' (see p.77).

In saying this are they referring to social gerontology as a discipline or as a field of study? Whatever is implied, educational gerontology is no more a subset of social gerontology than are economics, biology, sociology or social psychology. Like all these subjects educational gerontology draws upon a range of disciplines in order to offer insight into an area of social phenomena which has defined boundaries, even if they are not exactly precise.

Peterson's definition is very helpful, in the sense that he perceives that there is a relationship between adult education and gerontology. We have endeavoured to indicate this in the commentary on Figure 1. Clearly, education for older adults is within the continuum of what is called 'lifelong learning', certainly in the American sense (Peterson, 1976: p.63; Glendenning, 1990: pp.13-14; 1997: p.86).

Further, any endeavour concerning education for older adults must be conducted from within the parameters of adult education practice. Moreover, within the context of teaching gerontology, in all its variety, teaching methodology should be informed by adult education. In writing about her own professional gerontology course at Keele University, Bernard wrote: 'what we have tried to do with the Keele courses is to develop some of the most positive features of good adult education' (Bernard, 1995: p.93) and 'it requires tutors who are willing to expose their views and teaching styles to the gaze of colleagues as well as students' (p.98).

The question of disciplines

There is a further issue as to which discipline educational gerontology belongs, if any at all. Sherron and Lumsden have already indicated their preference for social gerontology. Withnall, on the other hand, has suggested that 'educational gerontology of the future may need to be subsumed within the developing philosophy of adult education as a lifelong process' (Withnall, 1992: p.23). Battersby has rejected this view on the grounds that one of the many failures of the functionalist paradigm has been the silence of the educators and facilitators of third age learning themselves. 'It is the sum of experiences, stories, reminiscences and practices of those educators working with older adults that should provide the narrative against which the various emergent philosophies should be examined ... [because it is the functionalist paradigm itself] which has tended to exclude the views of practitioners about aims, purposes, principles and practices of education in later life' (Battersby, 1993: p.20). Rather than give way to the hegemony of adult education philosophy, it is more beneficial to find ways of bringing educators together so that their dialogue about their professional practice might be activated as was proposed in chapter 2.

It is necessary, nevertheless, to see educational gerontology (EG) as of necessity being closely related to social gerontology and to adult education. Then more easily gerontological education may be seen as a sub-set of EG.

Because of its multidisciplinary nature, it is arguable whether we can refer to gerontology as being a discipline, nor is it 'a developing science', as was claimed by Wood et al. (1989: p.163). A scientific discipline is based on defined methods of investigation of identifiable and classified phenomena, thus specifying acceptable criteria for the validation of outcomes. As far as social gerontology is concerned, a Canadian sociologist has suggested that: 'Since the 1950s, knowledge components of social gerontology have evolved from three perspectives: (1) studies concerned with programmes of welfare and social policies for older people; (2) studies by social scientists who were primarily interested in using age to gain a better understanding of social behaviour in genera; and (3) studies by social scientists whose main objective was to understand and explain the ageing process and the status and behaviour of older people. All these groups began to label themselves as social gerontologists, in addition to their identification with other disciplines (sic), such as psychology, sociology, anthropology, political science or economics' (McPherson, 1990: p.14).

We can be certain that no one can master simultaneously the theory and methods of the biological, medical, anthropological, behavioural and social science disciplines which are relevant to the study of later life and demonstrate that mastery in personal research, although Peace has argued that 'we now have a body of research of sufficient calibre to begin to demonstrate which methods, or combinations of methods are most effective in particular circumstances' (Peace, 1990: p.5). This may also apply to those with professional training who become social gerontologists after having practised as qualified nurses, social workers, clinical psychologists and social administrators.

All these fields of study contribute to gerontology in juxtaposition rather than through interaction. It is then not difficult to recognize social gerontology as an arena of research and professional practice. But this is not the same as being a discipline, yet.

Competence in social gerontology

Then, it is a matter of some importance to consider whether it is possible to be actively involved in facilitating third age learning without competence in social gerontology. Is it possible, for example, to become involved in critical educational gerontology (CEG) without an awareness of the socio-economic developments which have contributed to the structured dependence of older people? This remains the same for tutors and facilitators as it does for older people themselves. Consciousness-raising is seen as being essential for the liberation and empowerment of older people and that is why perceiving education for older adults as being at the interface of social gerontology and adult education is a vital concept.

When however, we read the words of the editor of *The Older Adult as Learner*: 'Few of the contributors to this book are gerontologists *per se* ... I believe that this is a blessing, not a bane. Each contributor is a scholar in a given field ... Much more than this, each has, over the years, spent considerable time, either conducting research or administering programs for the elderly' (Lumsden 1985: p.xii), it is difficult to assess the gerontological competence of the authors, without knowing precisely their prior interest in and involvement with older people. There are no clues in the brief list of contributors and it is clearly wise not to be dogmatic and categorical about this.

But at the very least, those who are involved actively with older people as leaders or as dedicated members of the peer group should have received a certain standard of training in order to recognise from where the third age learners are coming. An obvious example is the field of advocacy, which requires advocates who are fluent in their understanding of pensions, benefits and the provision of care.

Conclusion

In conclusion then, we can say this: educational gerontology stands as a promising and exciting frontier. We have seen how there should indeed be an interaction between adult education and social gerontology. Educational gerontology and social gerontology need one another. But that is not the same as saying that educational gerontology is 'a legitimate and academically respectable branch of social gerontology' (Sherron and Lumsden, 1990: p.xi). This statement has more enthusiasm than substance.

Adult education is essential both to social and to educational gerontology. That is different from claiming that educational gerontology is any kind of 'branch'. Time will tell!

8　The debate continues: integrating educational gerontology with lifelong learning

Alexandra Withnall

... there really is an unfinished debate here and a way must be found of beginning to establish a theory about education for older adults which faces in a rigorous way the difficult questions that are raised. We can no longer be content to rely on anecdotal evidence and self-evaluation, as has been the case in the UK until now (Glendenning, 1997: p.90).

Introduction

The dawn of a new millenium seems an appropriate time to re-visit the debate about purpose in the education and training of older people, especially in view of the current political emphasis on lifelong learning, not just in the United Kingdom, but at an international level as well. How does education in later life relate to notions of lifelong learning? In the present climate, is it possible or even desirable to establish a theory about education for older adults? This chapter begins with a critical examination of the present UK government's vision of lifelong learning set out within a series of official publications. It then briefly summarises the 'unfinished debate' of the last few years concerning the philosophical and emerging theoretical approaches to the education of people who are post-work, in the sense that they are no longer primarily involved in earning a living or with major family responsibilities. Finally, an attempt is made to move the debate forward by arguing for a new perspective through a focus on lifelong learning itself.

Lifelong learning: the policy context

Notions of the individual and collective responsibility to continue learning throughout life are by no means new. They appear in different versions in the writings of Plato; in early Chinese philosophy; in the work of Comenius; and are implicit within the Jewish faith. Yet lifelong learning, as it is understood at the turn of the 20th century, appears to have adopted yet another new guise. For example, Edwards (1997) takes as his starting point the view that in late modernity, change and uncertainty are often seen as defining characteristics of the contemporary world. He argues that different forms of change - economic, cultural, technological and demographic - have been used to promote certain priorities within a generalised growth of interest in the concept of lifelong learning. He shows how these different analyses have been welded together by a variety of interests to produce a powerful discourse which has been influential in stressing the need for lifelong learning policies to support the need for economic competitivness. Indeed, a detailed analysis of three major policy reports related to the development of lifelong learning in the UK (Kennedy, 1997; National Committee of Inquiry into Higher Education, 1997; Fryer, 1997) reveals a strong priority accorded to vocational education and training in spite of some general rhetoric about the non-economic, personal and social benefits of lifelong learning (Tight, 1998).

The Green Paper *The Learning Age: a Renaissance for a New Britain* (1998) which drew partially on these reports, did emphasise the importance of developing a learning culture which would encourage personal independence, creativity and innovation and addressed the notion of the family and community as sites for learning. However, it conspicuously failed to develop an overall coherent philosophy of lifelong learning and it is notable that older people were generally ignored in the debate. Following the vision outlined in the Green Paper, the Government set out its proposals for a new framework for education and training of people over the age of 16 (other than those in higher education) in the White Paper *Learning to Succeed* (Cmd 4932, DfEE, 1999). Here it is acknowledged that the proposed new Learning and Skills Council will be expected to work with others in order to champion lifelong learning and to promote learning to 'men and women of all ages, including older people ...'. It is claimed that older people 'benefit greatly from learning' and that 'research has shown that older people who continue to be active learners enjoy healthier lifestyles and maintain their independence longer than those who stop learning' (p.55). The source of the evidence for this assertion is not given. There is also a somewhat patronising assumption as to the role which grandparents might play in family learning 'supporting children to acquire good reading skills' although there are no suggestions as to how this might be accomplished! This seems to posit a different role for older people than that advocated in the previous sentence. But can we really assume that older people would wish to have this kind of involvement? Would they receive training? Would there be opportunities to develop their own reading and other basic skills? These questions are not addressed. However, it is hastily emphasised that the proposed new Council will work to break down barriers to older people playing a full part in a learning society.

Although the White Paper at least acknowledges the need to consider the post-work population in its proposals, its rhetoric seems vague and presumptuous. The measures proposed to build opportunities for learning in the community for adults in general (Chapter 7), presumably designed to be more inclusive, are woolly and only address issues of re-motivation and re-engagement in terms of 'those who have few, if any qualifications' (p.60). This statement again suggests a vocational focus. Yet we know that many older learners who may not have qualifications do not necessarily wish to gain them. Even if they do, there are still problems. Notably, individual learning accounts, a key addition to the package of support available to adult learners and a major strand in the Government's lifelong learning strategy will only be available to 'people in work or those about to enter work' (p.57). Once again, people who are post-work are not genuinely part of the vision. Indeed, older people are frequently marginalised in educational policy circles by continued emphasis on economic competitiveness in tandem with a moral panic about the financial support of an ageing population which, although of major importance, tends to conceptualise later life as primarily a social problem.

Philosophical issues in the education and training of older adults

But why *should* older people merit consideration? What justification might there be for advocating a policy which recognises members of the post-work population as worthy of inclusion?

Let us now return to a consideration of the somewhat limited number of attempts which have been made to address philosophical issues concerning aspects of older people's education and training activities. A brief review by Withnall and Percy (1994) suggested that these have been located largely within a functionalist paradigm and derive mainly from activity theory and from sociological theories of role change (Havighurst, 1963). The emphasis in approaches which utilise role theory, as in activity theory, whether stated explicity or implicitly, is that older people must deal with role loss and adjustment to role change in retirement. Thus, the purpose of educational activity in later life is to provide solutions to the problem of how to achieve 'successful' ageing through the preservation of 'middle aged' attitudes or through adaptation to a socially acceptable role. It is assumed that education will contribute to this process by assuring good health, well-being and personal satisfaction in later life. This might be achieved through involvement in organised activity with others, through exercising the brain or through the nature of what is studied, especially learning which purports to offer opportunities for self-development - although Walker (1998) believes that this term requires further exploration. Writers such as Moody (1990) advocate that what is studied should facilitate self-reflection and life review, leading to a tranquil acceptance of human existence as finite, a view which is discussed further later in this chapter. To these ends, any debate has tended to be framed in terms of participation or non-participation in formally organised educational activities (Withnall and Percy, 1994), together with discussion of appropriate provision for older people as one of a range of identified target groups often seen as 'disadvantaged' (eg McGivney, 1990). It has found practical expression in the current *Older and Bolder* national development project run in England and Wales under the auspices of the National Institute for Adult Continuing Education (NIACE). To date, the initiative has utilised a mixture of statistical and anecdotal evidence to make a strong case for increasing public investment in learning provision for older people (Carlton and Soulsby, 1999). Other initiatives along similar lines are described in Schuller and Bostyn (1992) in their work for the Carnegie Inquiry into the Third Age - and, of course, it is this kind of thinking which has apparently encouraged the hasty inclusion of older people in Government plans for the development of its lifelong learning strategy! Certainly, there is now some preliminary medical evidence concerning the beneficial results of continued mental stimulation in later life with regard to the maintenance of good health (see a summary by Khaw, 1997). More relevant perhaps, are some recent findings from neurological research. Kotulak (1997), for example, reports that, whilst most research in this area has focused on the effects of early educational experiences on later life capabilities, there is now some evidence that mental training in later life can boost intellectual power, assist in maintaining mental function and help to reverse memory decline. Contrary to cellular theories of ageing (and conventional wisdom), he suggests that we do not lose brain cells as we age but rather that the brain's functions may become 'rusty' through disuse. In spite of somewhat extravagant claims about the health benefits of learning in later life and the need for enhanced educational provision, little of this work has been seriously considered by educational gerontologists during the last 20 years.

In addition to supposed health benefits, it is rather more the case that much of the published work to date is underpinned by an emphasis on older people's *rights* to have access to educational opportunities, often derived from notions of relative deprivation and what Townsend (1981) and others have described as the 'structured dependency' characteristic of later life. This approach can be discerned in Midwinter's moral arguments (1993) and in Schuller and Bostyn's contention that older people are entitled to educational opportunities as compensation for lack of these earlier in their lives, especially since the divides of gender and class have had such a major impact on the distibution of educational opportunities (1992). This argument also formed the basis of the 'educational charter for the elderly' published by Laslett (1984) who was closely involved in the genesis of the Forum on the Rights of Elderly People to Education (FREE) and the University of the Third Age (U3A) in the early 1980s. The *Older and Bolder* project has also made a strong case for recognition of older people's rights (Carlton and Soulsby, 1999).

Examining these kinds of arguments, Withnall and Percy (1994) called for something more than just a recognition of educational rights advocated from a quasi-political stance in which reasoning is grounded in concepts of equality and justice. They suggested that notions of equal opportunities, in the commonly accepted sense of the same opportunities for all, be abandoned in favour of a focus on the importance of human dignity; on the fulfilment of human potential and the promotion of fair treatment for everyone. More recently, Elmore (1999) has examined this moral dimension further through a closely reasoned advocacy of older people's access to both instrumental and expressive education on the basis of social justice, using notions of fair equality of opportunity, access to democratic participation and the status of equal citizenship at a time when Western society is undergoing fundamental change in its social and economic structure. In these ways, educational gerontology becomes an indispensable tool of liberal democracy.

A further philosophical approach which found expression in the *1993 European Year of Older People and Solidarity Between Generations* and within which is located the Government's vision of grandparents as participants in family learning, is that of intergenerational recognition and reciprocity. Such an approach can be traced to the theories of developmental psychologists such as Erikson (1963) and Levinson (1978), although the proponents of this approach would be unlikely to acknowledge this derivation. Laslett (1989) for example, argues that self-fulfilment in later life implies older people taking responsibility for themselves and their learning and also recognising the obligation to create an interchange with younger members of society, so that an equitable relationship with the future can be secured for the whole of society. The theme of generativity in later life also underpins the exploratory work of Friedan (1993) and, unconsciously, informs much of the practical intergenerational work taking place in different countries, notably in the United States. However, theories of adult development and the personality changes taking place in adulthood which see progression in 'stages' passing through a phase of seeking intergenerational understanding in 'late middle age' and culminating in a final stage of recognition and self-fulfilment through review and acceptance (see Moody, 1990, discussed above) can be criticised on the grounds that the sheer diversity of experience in adult life makes it impossible to predict major stages. Stage theories also imply a discontinuity of development, whilst other psychological theories stress the continuity of personality during adulthood. It may be, therefore, that whilst educational intergenerational activity might be relevant and rewarding for some older people, it needs further debate and exploration and cannot be regarded as always appropriate and relevant for all.

Theoretical issues: critical educational gerontology

It can be argued that, at present, none of these existing approaches to education in later life deals adequately with the impact of the social structure nor with the historical and cultural contexts in which ageing takes place. However, the 1980s saw the emergence of a range of critical perspectives within the field of social gerontology (Phillipson, 1998). These have also begun to influence debates in the field of educational gerontology, especially the development of the idea of a critical educational gerontology. Glendenning, a staunch advocate of the need for a new approach for over ten years (see Chapter 2) described succinctly in a review essay nearly ten years ago how he saw the role of this new kind of gerontology:

> Critical educational gerontology would encourage tutors and students to examine the relation between knowledge and power and control. It would enable education to be seen as an agent of social change, as it was by the early exponents of the University of the Third Age in France. It would take into account the conflicting messages that we receive about the learning characteristics of older people. We also need clear answers to a number of questions. Among them are: Whose interests are being served? Why do we need education for older adults? ... Should we not be questioning existing practices and models of education for older adults or are we content? (Glendenning 1991: 11, pp.215-16).

Glendenning has raised these kinds of questions on several occasions since 1991, most recently emphasising that critical educational gerontology would also assert that life experiences have been and continue to be a learning process and that reflection on these processes can be liberating. He argues that critical educational gerontology 'seeks to unmask conflicts and contradictions that lie behind a superficial harmony of ideas'. He asks why some people claim that 'education is good for people' and that 'quality of life is enhanced by education'. The problem, he asserts, is that educational provision for older adults is still shackled to the functionalist paradigm as we have mentioned above. What is required, he suggests, is a more robust paradigm where a new discourse about later life might

92

be located. He sees a real need firstly, to disentangle the reasons for the marginalisation and structured dependency of older people; and secondly, for education to lead older people to take charge of their lives and to become emancipated, thereby introducing a new moral dimension to the debate about educational purpose in later life (Glendenning, 1997: p.88). That his ideas are beginning to resonate with educators of adults can be seen in some examples of how the possibilities of critical educational gerontology are being explored in practice (see especially Chapter 6, this volume).

Glendenning may be correct in his insistence on the need for a new paradigm within which to explore major questions concerning later life education. However, it can be argued, as Usher at al (1997) have done, that although an approach derived from critical theory seeks to unmask distortions and constraints, it actually runs the risk of substituting a partial and somewhat distorted view of human experience - and indeed the drive for emancipation and empowerment may itself become oppressive.

Certainly, later life is increasingly characterised by widening inequalities determined to a large degree by the socio-economic structure and the growth of consumerism permeated by sexual politics and by issues of class, race, ethnicity and age itself. Psychological evidence concerning the impact of ageing on health status, intellectual skills and lifestyles (Stuart-Hamilton, 1994; Slater, 1998) also suggests a sharper division between the fit and active majority and the minority suffering acute or chronic illness whether mental, physical or both. But to assume a heterogeneity among older people, uniformly disadvantaged and committed to praxis is simply to impose a new kind of ideological constraint. Such an approach may also assume a desire and an ability among educators of adults to institute critical dialogue, to be themselves unconstrained by ideological or personal beliefs and to be committed to social action. In addition, critical educational gerontology leaves no room for the expressive educational activities which older people may successfully organise for themselves and, in its emphasis on *education per se* seems to ignore the possibilities presented by a concept of *learning* in later life whether in formal or informal situations. Indeed, it appears to this writer that the issues to be explored are more complex than have been acknowledged so far.

Rethinking lifelong learning and learning post-work

It has been seen that, apart from the work of Glendenning, educational gerontology in the UK is largely atheoretical. An alternative formulation which seems to offer a way forward would be to focus on *learning*, as suggested above, rather than on *education in later life* and to begin from the proposition that, in late modernity, a conceptualisation of lifelong learning to emphasise 'a cradle to grave' concept which really stresses vocational education and training and makes only a vague reference to older people, is inadequate. Learning might be more readily located in social and cultural developments such as the growth of consumerism and in a range of social practices (Usher et al., 1997). Indeed, Gilleard (1996) among others, argues that contemporary consumer culture plays a part in helping older people to shape their identities in later life at a time when the meaning of growing old is subject to revision at a time of rapid change. In this sense, formally provided learning opportunities for adults generally have themselves become part of the consumer culture, offering the promise of access to a particular (better) lifestyle and often marketed as 'fun' with enjoyment as the main aim. Yet most adults are well aware that there is little fun involved in the processes of learning itself. On the contrary, it is often challenging, demanding and even painful. However, the fun element may well be provided by the social context, the chance to spend time in the company of like-minded people, to subject oneself to new experiences, and perhaps to have a focal point to give structure to one's week.

A further point related to the above, is that, of course, learning does not have to take place in formally organised settings. The success of the University of the Third Age as it has developed in Britiain and elsewhere and, indeed, other similar informal and self-help endeavours has shown that older people do not necesarily wish to buy into a lifestyle but that other factors, described above, may be important in helping them to shape a post work identity. Learning may also be incidental, unanticipated or imposed - Kupfermann's moving and illuminating account of how she was forced to learn to deal with a torrent of unfamiliar tasks after the death of her spouse is a case in point (1992). Or learning may well consist of the kind of reflection and life review which takes place spasmodically over time and which may lead to greater self-knowledge and insight (see Moody, above).

Phillipson (1998) in a penetrative analysis of changes to the context and experiences associated with growing old in late modernity suggests that later life is being reconstructed as a period of potential choice and opportunity, but also as an arena of risk and danger. Certainly, choice itself is always problematic and probably more so in later life. However, this kind of thinking suggests that we need to understand the basis on which older people make choices about undertaking learning in both formal and informal contexts in an uncertain world, to identify what constitutes a successful learning experience and to assess what learning means in the context of their own lives. The very heterogeneity of the post-work population further suggests that it is necessary to use their experiences as learners and to understand the influence of different events and beliefs over the life course. The questions to be asked might be summarised as follows:

How do older people themselves define and understand learning (and education) post work?

What value do older people place on learning (and on education)? What are the contexts and discourses over the life course which have shaped their perceptions?

How do they construct and develop ideas and attitudes to learning and to education?

What outcomes do formal/informal and other types of learning have for older people in the context of their own lives? How are these outcomes experienced and described?

Answers to these questions would also help us to reconsider Glendenning's proposition that education for older adults could be a potential force for social change - and indeed, might well help to increase the status and visibility of older adults within the community. Answers would also help to focus on a broader issue: what are the implications for social and educational policies in general in repect of a stronger emphasis on learning in later life? What would a life course approach entail? Such a perspective suggests that learning activity post-work and the forms that it might take at different periods is influenced by a complex interplay of a range of individual characteristics and by a variety of individual and collective experiences over a lifetime. Analysis of these needs to be combined with an exploration of differing situational experiences, opportunities and constraints throughout the life course including the post-work period. Such an approach offers a distinctive perspective on the factors which might influence older people to continue or to take up learning activity at any stage of their post work lives. It also provides a way of investigating the relationship between learning undertaken in formal or in informal contexts and encourages reflection on that learning which is unintentional or unanticipated.

The life course approach would also help to illuminate how the constraints (or opportunities) of age, class, gender, race, location etc. may combine with other factors to influence learning choices and activities in later life. Jarvis (1994) has begun to address some of these issues by theorizing about the relationship between biography and experience and Jamieson et al. (1998) have adopted a life course perspective in a small qualitative study of a group of older people attending a residential summer school. Although the latter were able to offer a basic framework for understanding education in the context of retirement, they admit that their study focused on a small and atypical group of older people.

What is now required is the development and testing of a conceptual model of the reasons for participation in, pathways through, and outcomes of

95

undertaking different types of learning activity post-work. Research of this kind would also enable us not only to identify the circumstances which affect opportunity and choice for learning at different points of later life but would also give us a clearer understanding of older people's experiences as learners in a variety of settings, informal as well as formal. Then we may be able to move towards a refinement and re-alignment of theory in lifelong learning by taking a more inclusive perspective; and to consider the implications for social and educational policies in general in respect of a stronger emphasis on learning in later life. In this way, educational gerontology might be integrated within a new theoretical perspective on lifelong learning itself.

Researching learning with older people

In advocating the use of empirically-derived data from which to begin theory-building, a comment must be made about the use of personal experience methods. In asking older people to reflect upon their life histories and present learning experiences, it has to be recognized that this method is not without its own particular problems. It is generally acknowledged by those who advocate the life course method that the self cannot be a single stable identity and that subjectivity is always changing so that biographical accounts may take on different meanings at different times. At the same time, ageing confronts late modern assumptions of continual change and re-invention of the self with something of a dilemma since, although people may age in diverse ways, everyone faces the same ultimate finitude of existence. However, any empirical research needs to be carried out, then, with an acknowledgement that the topic under investigation, the subjects of the research and the changing perspectives of the researchers themselves may shape the way in which the research is reported and scripted and that strategies may need to adapt and evolve over time. In addition, as in any research, ethical isues need consideration. The issue of research as an enactment of power relations between researchers and the subjects of the research has perplexed educational and social science researchers for a considerable period of time (see Usher et al, 1997 for a detailed discussion). One way to begin to confront this would be to encourage older people to undertake research themselves. Organisations such as the Senior Studies Institute at the University of Strathclyde and the Pre-Retirement Association together with some U3A branches have already developed considerable expertise in training members to carry out research. However, the informed consent of research informants, assurances of anonymity and issues concerned with research ownership would still need detailed thought and discussion.

Concluding remarks

This chapter has attempted, firstly, to comment critically on the paucity of the current UK Government's current vision of lifelong learning - a perspective which has little to say about the post-work population's role and involvement. Secondly, it has reviewed a range of statements about purpose in the education of older adults. It may well be the case that all of these can be justified at any one time to the extent that they are not viewed as exclusive ideologies. Thirdly, it has been suggested that a novel way forward would be to change the emphasis from thinking about *education* to *learning* and that the involvement of older people in learning whether in formal or informal contexts, needs to be located and justified within a life course perspective which would acknowledge the heterogeneity of the post-work population. In obtaining empirical data, however, we need a new research paradigm which would place ageing itself at the centre of debate and which would acknowledge that *learning* is something which the individual continues to do throughout life. To talk purely of *education* in later life seems to assume involvement with the entire panoply of formally organised provision and a lack of control over the processes. In these ways,we might be enabled to develop a new and meaningful theory of lifelong learning which would incorporate the post-work population both for a new century and for succeeding generations as they grow older.

9 Teaching and learning in later life: considerations for the future

The purpose of this book has been to raise awareness that the so-called 'education for older adults movement' has been predicated on an inadequate paradigm. It was suggested earlier that the failure to achieve legitimation for mainstream educational provision for older persons may very well have been the result of there being no recognisably theoretical basis for this work on a par with the generally accepted theories of education. A taxonomy of third age education has not been adequately developed anywhere in the world and this is long overdue.

Some will always argue that such a development would be counter-productive because it would be divisive, although from a German perspective, Rosemayr (1983) has argued that the old educational models are simply not adequate for what he termed the 'late freedom' that we have in later life. They are certainly hopeless for those who completed their secondary schooling at an early age as we have noted previously. But to search for a taxonomy and a new paradigm is not divisive in our view. It is an honest attempt to recognise reality and as Lowy has said, 'the movement to find a special terminology in many western countries points to a belief that education in the later years is quite different from traditional adult education' (Low and O'Connor, 1986: p.11).

Pierre Brasseul reflecting on the experiences of the U3As in France, which had no tradition of formalised adult education as in Britain, suggested that older adults responded to the restrictions of the laws which confined educational opportunities in the 1970s to those in the active workforce and as a result organised their own unofficial educational opportunities: *universités du troisième âge* (Universities of the Third Age):

Its greatest originality ... lies in the way in which it brings together the joy of learning and the pleasure of teaching, at a time when official education is characterised by a certain gloominess (Brasseul, 1985: p.2).

The U3As soon opened their doors to younger adults, particularly those who were free and able to study during the day. Eventually this interaction between young and old created a climate in which the retired were able to participate in traditional courses as well. However their motivations were generally not work-related and this broadened the scope and purpose of education in France:

Consequently, education takes on another meaning. It is linked to the person and no longer to production, to the 'being' and no longer 'the doing'. It is also this which explains why there is no longer a time limit. This type of education goes on for a lifetime (Brasseul, 1985: p.5).

Brasseul went on to say that this revolution was not as new as it might have seemed. It was rather a return to the pre-industrial goal of education, which, however, was directed at the leisure class. Now, as leisure was becoming a common experience in the developed countries, education for leisure and education directed at the development of the individual added an important new dimension to the meaning of education for *all* adults. It was then inevitable that the French U3As in some instances took on the complexion of 'clubs for the retired'.

In Britain in the 1970s and 1980s there was often open opposition from adult educators to what they regarded as age segregation in mainstream adult education and there was even hostility in some quarters that the issue should be raised at all. It is not proposed to protract this particular argument here. It was dealt with in chapter one of this volume. But simply to suggest that Walker's view that there is a parallel here with the women's movement is correct. For out of the women's movement emerged a greater consciousness concerning women's potential, compared to their contemporary roles just as there has emerged in the last two decades a demand for education and training for new roles and participation in society for those in late life (Walker, 1996, p.52). She cites Manheimer and Snodgrass (1993) as saying:

... today's older adults may be seeking pathways to new roles and new identities through renewal of the learning process and direction towards possible volunteer and entrepreneurial opportunities ... linked to the older person's choice to stay or get involved in the community (p.586).

Walker continues:

Education for the third age is happening and will continue due to consumer demand and the recognition of new markets for educational services. Educators and other human service practitioners will increasingly be called upon to work in an educational mode with older frailer people (Walker, 1996, p.140).

We have then in this volume attempted to consider what we regard as the principal topics which must be confronted in the future: the education of older persons as a moral right; the importance of applying critical theory to any developing theory of third age education and the empirical finding that education in later life leads to unquestioned empowerment of the older person as older people search for their place and identity in a postmodern world. We have also noted the lack of theory to guide professionals who are seeking to transfer responsibility for decision-making to older people themselves thus enabling them to assume more effective leadership roles.

It has been argued that what is required is nothing less than a new paradigm because we regard the old functional paradigm as empty and hanging in the wind, because it depends entirely on the self-reported musings of teachers and learners alike. Much work will be required in the future to counter the claims of the functionalists that education is good for older people and enhances their quality of life by improving their health and sense of well-being and self-esteem. Much controlled research will be required before this can be validated. Similarly, the often quoted assertion that it is an economic investment because educated persons in later life are less likely to be in need of costly institutional care. No instruments exist which can enable us to demonstrate this, although Withnall has indicated that this situation may be changing.

It has also been argued in these pages that we need to recognise a much closer relationship between social and educational gerontology. Educational Gerontology, especially critical educational gerontology still has questions to answer as Withnall again has pointed out in the previous chapter on 'the unfinished debate'.

Withnall has urged that for her as a adult education researcher as well as a social gerontologist, it is essential to rethink the relation between lifelong learning and learning post-work, and that it may be fruitful to centre our attention more on *learning* rather than *education*. She has proposed in chapter 8 that it might be beneficial to shift the discussion from later life altogether and to locate and justify education for older people within a life course perspective. In her endeavour to reposition what she calls 'the unfinished debate', she has pointed out that learning post-work takes different forms at different periods because it is influenced by 'a complex interplay of a range of individual characteristics and by a variety of individual and collective experiences over a lifetime' (page 95 above). An analysis of this interplay might well illuminate how a life course approach might better enable us to integrate 'educational gerontology' (in the restricted mode of matters relating to education in later life) within a new theoretical perspective on *lifelong learning* itself. So many times in the recent past we have been confused by the limited meaning that has been placed upon the term in official government statements, as has been mentioned numerous times in this collection of essays.

Rather than merely searching for a new paradigm for education for older adults, what has emerged in these pages is the need for a new paradigm for lifelong learning itself, which would place ageing at the centre of the debate. It is our hope that these essays may provide a number of building blocks which may enable this to happen in the future, so that we may confidently present an argument which implies that lifelong education really means that education is a basic right at any age. This merely confirms what the excellent Carlton and Soulsby (1999) reiterate in *Learning to Grow Older and Bolder*, in exceptional detail.

References

Abrams, M. (1981), 'Education and later life', *Research Perspectives on Ageing*, Mitcham: Age Concern Research Unit.

Agruso, V.M. (1978), *Learning in the Later Years: Principles of Educational Gerontology*, New York: Academic Press.

Allman, P. (1984), 'Self-help learning and its relevance for learning and development in later life', in E. Midwinter (ed.), *op.cit.*

Arber, S. And Ginn, J. (1991), 'Gender, class and income inequalities in later life', *British Journal of Sociology*, 42(3), pp.369-96.

Audit Commission (1986), *Making a Reality of Community Care*, London: HMSO.

Baars, J. (1991), 'The challenge of critical studies', *Journal of Aging Studies*, 5.(3): 219-43.

Battersby, D. (1987), 'From Andragogy to Gerogogy', *Journal of Educational Gerontology*, 2(12), pp.4-10.

Battersby, D. (1993), 'Developing an epistemology of professional practice within Educational Gerontology', *Journal of Educational Gerontology*, 8(1), pp.17-25.

Baumann, Z. (1992), *Intimations of Postmodernity*, London: Routledge and Kegan Paul.

Beck, U. (1992), *Risk Society*, London: Sage Publications.

Bengston, V. and Achenbaum, V.W. (eds) (1993), *The Changing Contract Across Generations*. New York: Aldine de Gruyter.

Bernard, M. (1998), 'Taking charge - strategies for self-empowered health behaviour among older people', *Health Education Journal*, 47(pp.2-3).

Bernard, M. and Phillips, J. (1998), *The Social Policy of Old Age: Moving into the 21st Century*, London: Centre for Policy on Ageing.

Biggs, S. (1993), *Understanding Ageing*, Buckingham: Open University Press.

Biggs, S. (1997), 'Choosing not to be old? Masks, bodies and identity management in later life', *Ageing and Society*, 17(5): pp.553-70.

Bond, J., Coleman, P. and Peace, S. (1993), *Ageing in Society: An Introduction to Social Gerontology*, London: Sage Publications.

Bourdieu, P. (1974), The school as a conservative force', in J. Eggleston (ed.), *Contemporary Research in the Sociology of Education*, London: Metheuen.

Brasseul. P. (1984), 'Senior citizens challenge traditional education: the French experience, *Educational Gerontology*, 10 (3) pp.185-96.

Brink, S. (1993), 'Elderly empowerment', *U.S. News and World Report*, vol. 114, pt. 16, pp.65-66.

Bromley, D.B. (1988), *Human Ageing: An Introduction to Gerontology*, Harmondsworth: Penguin.

Brookfield, S. (1989), *Developing Critical Thinkers*, Jossey Bass, San Francisco.

Bytheway, B. (1995), *Ageism*, Buckingham: Open University Press.

Butler, R.N. (1975), *Why Survive? Growing Old in America*, New York: Harper and Row.

Carlton, S. and Soulsby, J. (1999), *Learning to Grow Older and Bolder*, Leicester: NIACE.

Clarke, P.G. (1987), 'Individual autonomy, cooperative empowerment and planning for long-term care decision making', *Journal of Aging Studies*, 1, pp.65-76.

Cole, T. (1992), *The Journey of Life*. Cambridge: Cambridge University Press.

Cole, T., van Tassell, D. and Kastenbaum, R. (eds) (1992), *Handbook of the Humanities and Ageing*, New York: Springer Publishing Company.

Cole, T., Achenbaum, A., Jakobi, P. and Kastenbaum, R. (eds) (1993), *Voices and Visions of Ageing: Toward a Critical Gerontology*, New York: Springer Publishing Company.

Coleman, A. (ed. J. Groombridge) (1982), *Preparation for Retirement in England and Wales*, Leicester: National Institute of Adult Education.

Cox, E.O. and Parsons, R.J. (1994), *Empowerment-oriented Social Work Practice with the Elderly*, Brooks/Cole., Pacific Grove, CA.

Cumming, E. and Henry, W.R. (1966), *Growing Old: The Process of Disengagement*, New York: Basic Books.

Cusack, S.A. (1998), 'Leadership in seniors centres: Power and empowerment in the relations between seniors and staff', *Education and Ageing*, 6(1), pp.41-58.

Cusack, S.A. (2000, in process), 'Research as Emancipatory Education: A method with attitude for creating a new old age', in K. Percy (ed.), *Untitled Monograph*, Aldershot: Ashgate.

Cusack, S. and Thompson, W. (1995), *Leadership for the 90s: A Program to Train Seniors to Facilitate Leadership*, Summary Report of a Leadership

Project sponsored by the Dogwood Pavilion Association, City of Coquitlam, and funded by New Horizons, Health Canada.

Cusack, S.A. and Thompson, W.J.A (1997), 'Building a Community of Leaders: Research and development of a program to train seniors as empowering leaders', *Canadian Journal for Studies in Adult Education*, 10(2), pp.19-36.

Cusack, S.A. and Thompson, W.J.A. (1998), *Leadership in Retirement: Aging with Purpose and Passion*, Taylor and Francis/Bruner Mazell, Philadelphia.

Cusack, S.A. and Thompson, W.J.A. (1998a), 'Mental fitness: developing a vital aging society', *Men sana in corpose sano*, International Journal of Lifelong Learning. 17, pp.307-17.

Cusack, S.A. and Thompson, W.J.A. (1998b), *Mental Fitness: The Continuing Experience*, Summary Report of Phase IV in the Research and Development of Mental Fitness Programs. Submitted to the Lifelong Learning Committee, Century House Association, New Westminster, BC, Canada.

Daniels, N. (1996), *Justice and Justification: Reflective Equilibrium in Theory and Practice*, Cambridge University Press, New York and London.

Decalmer, P. and Glendenning, F. (eds) (1997), *The Mistreatment of Elderly People*, 2nd edition, London: Sage Publications.

Department of Education and Employment (DfEE) (1995), *Lifetime Learning: a Consultation Document*, London: HMSO.

Department of Education and Employment (1998), *National Adult Learning Survey*, London: DfEE.

Donahue, W.T. (1955) (ed.), *Education for Late Maturity*, New York: Whitesidde.

Du Zicai (1994), 'The China Association of Universities for the Aged', *Education and Ageing*, 10 (2) pp.115-6.

Du Zicai (1998), 'Education for older people in China', *Education and Ageing*, 13 (2) pp.186-8.

Dworkin, R. (1972), *Taking Rights Seriously*, Duckworth, London.

Dychtwald, K. (1997), 'Wake-up call: The 10 physical, social, spiritual, economic and political crises the boomers will face as they age in the 21st Century', in M. Freedman (ed.) *Critical Issues in Aging, No. 1*, pp. 11-13. An Annual Magazine of the American Society on Aging, American Society on Aging, San Francisco, CA.

Edwards, R. (1998), *Changing Places?* London: Routledge.

Elias, J.I. and Merriam, S. (1980), *Philosophical Foundations of Adult Education*, Huntington, N.Y.: Krieger.

Ensor, R.C.K. (1950), 'The problem of quantity and quality in the British population', *Eugenics Review*, Vol.13(3).

Erikson, E. (1963), *Childhood and Society*, 2nd edition, New York: Norton.

Estes, C. (1979), *The Aging Enterprise*, San Francisco: Jossey Bass.

Estes, C. (1986), 'The politics of ageing', *Ageing and Society*, 6, pp.121-34.

Estes, C. (1991), 'The new political economy of ageing: introduction and critique', in M. Minkler and C. Estes, *Critical Perspectives on Ageing: The Political and Moral Economy of Growing Old*, New York: Baywood Publishing Company.

Estes, C. (1993), 'The aging enterprise revisited', *The Gerontologist*, 33: 292-8.

Estes, C. and Binney, E. (1989), 'The biomedicalisation of ageing: dangers and dilemmas', *The Gerontologist*, 29 (5), pp.587-98.

Eurolink Age Bulletin (1995), November, pp.9-10.

Evandrou, M. (1997), *Baby Boomers: Ageing into the 21st Century*, London: Age Concern England.

Evans, N. (1985), *Post-Education Society: Recognising Adults as Learners*, London: Croom Helm.

Featherstone, M. and Hepworth, M. (1989), 'Ageing and old age: Reflections on the postmodern life course', in B. Bytheway, T. Keil, P. Allat and A. Bryman (eds), *Becoming and Being Old*, London: Sage Publications.

Fennell, G., Phillipson, C. and Evers, H. (1989), *The Sociology of Old Age*, Milton Keynes: Open University Press.

Freire, P. (1972), *The Pedagogy of the Oppressed*, Harmondsworth: Penguin.

Friedan, B. (1993), *The Fountain of Age*, New York: Simon and Schuster.

Fryer, R. (1997), *Learning for the Twenty-First Century: first report of the National Advisory Group for Continuing Education and Lifelong Learning*, London:NAGCELL.

Gibson, R. (1986), *Critical Theory and Education*, London: Hodder and Stoughton.

Giddens, A. (1991), *Modernity and Self-Identity*, Oxford: Polity Press.

Gilleard, C. (1996), 'Consumption and identity in later life: towards a cultural gerontology', *Ageing and Society*, 16 (4) pp.489-98.

Glendenning, F. (1983), 'Educational Gerontology: a review of American and British Developments', *International Journal of Lifelong Education*, 2 (10), pp.63-82.

Glendenning, F. (1985), *Educational Gerontology: International Perspectives*, London: Croom Helm.

Glendenning, F. (1986), 'Lifelong education for the over-60s', in S. Jones (ed.) *Liberation of the Elders*, Stoke-on-Trent, Beth Johnson Foundation in association with Adult Education Department, University of Keele.

Glendennning, F. (1987), 'Educational gerontology in the future: unanswered questions', in S. Di Gregorio (ed.), *Social Gerontology: New Directions*, London: Croom Helm.

Glendenning, F. (1990), 'The emergence of educational gerontology', in F. Glendenning and K. Percy (eds), *op.cit.*

Glendenning, F. (1991), 'What is the future of educational gerontology?', *Ageing and Society*, 11, pp.209-16.

Glendenning, F. (1997), 'Why educational gerontology is not yet established as a field of study: some critical implications', *Education and Ageing*, vol. 12, nos. 1/2, November.

Glendenning, F. (1997), 'What is elder abuse and neglect?', in P. Decalmer and F. Glendenning (eds) *op.cit.*

Glendenning, F. and Percy. K. (eds) (1990), *Ageing, Education and Society: Readings in Educational Gerontology*, Keele: Association for Educational Gerontology.

Gramsci, A. (1971), *The Prison Notebooks*, London: Lawrence and Wishart.

Groombridge, B. (1982), 'Learning, education and later life', *Adult education*, 54 (4) pp.314-27.

Groombridge, B. (1989), 'Education and later life', in A.M. Warnes (ed.), *Human Ageing and Later Life*, London: Edward Arnold.

Groves, D. (1993), 'Work, poverty and older women', in M. Bernard and K. Meade (eds), *Women Come of Age*, London: Edward Arnold.

Gubrium, J.F. (1993), 'Voice and Context in a New Gerontology', in T. Cole, A. Achenbaum, P. Jakobi and R. Kastenbaum, R. (eds), *Voices and Visions of Aging: Toward a Critical Gerontology*, New York: Springer Publishing Company.

Guillemard, A-M. (ed.) (1983), *Old Age and the Welfare State*, New York: Sage Publications.

Harris, L. and Associates (1974), *The Myths and Realities of Aging in America*, Washington D.C.: National Council of Aging.

Harris, K. and Cole, W.E. (1980), *The Sociology of Ageing*, Boston: Houghton Miflin.

Harrison, R. (1988), 'Policy and practice in educational provision for older people', *Journal of Educational Gerontology*, 3 (1), pp.4-14.

Hatton, V. (1997), Southcare Wellness Center. Paper presented to a symposium, 'Empowering senior citizens around the world through education', 1997 World Congress of Gerontology, Adelaide, Australia, August 19-34.

Havighurst, R.J. (1963), 'Successful ageing' in R.H. Williams et al. (eds), *Processes of Aging* 1, New York: Atherton.

Havighurst, R.J. (1964), 'Changing status and roles during the adult life cycle: Significance for adult education', in H. Burns (ed.), *Sociological Backgrounds of Adult Education*, Chicago: Center for the Liberal Education of Adults.

Higgs, P. (1995), 'Citizenship and old age: the end of the road?', *Ageing and Society*, 15 (4), pp.535-50.

Hofland, B.F. (1994), 'When capacity fades and autonomy is constricted: a client-centered approach to residential care', *Generations*, vol. 18, pt. 4, pp.31-35.

Hunter, E. (ed.) (1982), *Education for Older People: a National Policy Framework*, Edinburgh: Scottish Basic Education Unit.

Jamieson, A., Miller, A. and Stafford, J. (1998), 'Education in a life course perspective: continuities and discontinuities', *Education and Ageing*, 13 (3), pp.213-28.

Jarvis, P. (1992), 'Learning, developing and ageing in late modernity', *Journal of Educational Gerontology*, 7 (1), pp.7-15.

Jessup, F.W. (ed.) (1969), *Lifelong Learning*, Oxford: Pergamon Press.

Johnson, H.R. (1980), 'Introduction' in C. Tibbitts, H. Friedsham, P. Kerschner and H. McLusky (eds), *Academic Gerontology: Dillemmas of the 1980s*, Michigan: University of Michigan.

Johnson, M. (1976), 'That was your life: a biographical approach to later life', in J.M.A. Munnichs, W.J.A. Van Den Heuvel (eds), *Dependency and Interdependency in Old Age*, Hague: Martinus Nijhoff.

Kaminsky, M. (1993), 'Definitional ceremonies: Depolitizing and reenchanting the culture of age', in T. Cole, W.A. Achenbaum, P. Jakobi, and R Kastenbaum (eds), *Voices and Visions of Aging*, New York: Springer Publishing Co.

Katz, S. (1996), *Disciplining Old Age*, Virginia: University Press of Virginia.

Kennedy, H.(1997), *Learning Works. Widening Participation in Further Education* (Kennedy Report), Coventry: Further Education Funding Council.

Khaw, K-T. (1997), 'Healthy ageing', *British Medical Journal*, Vol. 315, pp.1090-96.

Kenyon, C.M. (1996), 'Ethical issues in ageing and biography', *Ageing and Society*, 16(6): 659-76.

Knowles, M.S. (1984), *Andragogy in Action: Applying Modern Principles of Adult Learning*, San Francisco: Jossey-Bass.

Koller, M.R. (1968), *Social Gerontology*, New York: Random House.

Kornfeld, R. (1997). *Training the Elderly in Gerontology and its Integration Into Social Support Systems*, Paper presented to a symposium, 'Empowering senior citizens around the world through education', 1997 World Congress of Gerontology, Adelaide, Australia, August 19-34.

Kotulak, R. (1997), *Inside the Brain: Revolutionary Discoveries of How the Mind Works*, Kansas City: Andrews McMeel Publishing.

Kupfermann, J. (1992), *When the Crying's Done*, London: Robson Books.

Lash, S. and Urry, J. (1987), *The End of Organised Capitalism*, Cambridge: Polity Press.

Laslett, P. (1984), 'The education of the elderly in Britain', in E. Midwinter (ed.), *op.cit.*

Laslett, P. (1989), *A Fresh Map of Life*, London: Weidenfeild and Nicholson.

Leonard, P. (1984), *Personality and Ideology*, London: Macmillan.

Levine, M. L. (1988), *Age Discrimination and the Mandatory Retirement Controversy*, Johns Hopkins University Press, Baltimore and London.

Levinson, D.J. (1978), *The Seasons of a Man's Life*, New York: Ballantine Books.

Londoner, C.A. (1990), 'Instrumental and expressive education: A basis for needs assessment and planning', in R.H. Sherron and D.B. Lumsden, *op.cit.* 3rd edition, pp.85-108.

Loring, R.K. (1978) 'Foreword', in R.H. Sherron and D.B. Lumsden (eds), *op.cit.*

Lowy, L. and O'Connor D. (1986), *Why Education in the Later Years?*, New York: D.C. Heath and Co.

Lukes, S. (1982), *Power. A Radical View*, Macmillan, London.

Lumsden, D.B. (ed.) (1985), *The Older Adult as Learner: Aspects of Educational Gerontology*, Washington D.C.: Hemisphere.

Lynott, R. and Lynott, P.P. (1996), 'Tracing the course of theoretical development in the sociology of aging', *The Gerontologist*, 36(6), pp.749-60.

McPherson, B.D. (1990), *Aging as a Social Process: An Introduction to Individual and Population Ageing*, 2nd edition, Toronto: Butterworths.

McGivney, V. (1990), *Education's for Other People*, Leicester: NIACE.

Midwinter, E. (1982), *Age is Opportunity: Education and Older People*, London: Centre for Policy on Ageing.

Midwinter, E. (ed.) (1984), *Mutual Aid Universities*, London: Croom Helm.

Midwinter, E. (1993), 'Face-to-face provision and the older learner', in J.Calder (ed.) *Disaffection and Diversity: Overcoming Barriers for Adult Learners*, London: Falmer Press.

Minkler, M. (1985), 'Building supportive ties and sense of community among the inter-city elderly: The Tenderloin Senior Outreach Project', *Health Education Quarterly*, 12(4), pp.303-314.

Minkler, M. (1996), 'Critical perspectives on ageing: New challenges for gerontology', *Ageing and Society*, 16, pp.467-487.

Minkler, M. and Estes, C. (eds) (1991), *Critical Perspectives on Ageing*, New York: Baywood Publishing Inc.

Minkler, M. and Estes, C. (1997), *Critical Gerontology*, New York: Baywood Publishing.

Moody, H.R. (1988), *Abundance of Life: Human Development Policies for an Aging Society*, New York: Columbia University Press.

Moody, H.R. (1988), 'Toward a critical gerontology: The contribution of the humanities to theories of aging', in J.E. Birren and V.L. Bengston (eds), *Emergent Theories of Aging*, New York: Springer. pp.19-40.

Moody, H. (1990), 'Education and the life cycle: a philosophy of ageing', in R.H. Sherron and D.B. Lumsden (eds) *Introduction to Educational Gerontology*, New York: Hemisphere Publishing Corporation.

Moody, H.R. (1992), 'Gerontology and critical theory', *The Gerontologist*, 32(3): 294-295.

Moody, H.R. (1993), 'Overview: What is critical gerontology and why is it important?', in S.A. Bass, F.G. Caro and Yung-Pin Chen (eds), *Achieving a Productive Ageing Society*, Westport: Auburn House.

Moody, H.R. (1993), 'Overview: what is critical gerontology and why is it important', in T. Cole, A. Achenbaum, P. Jakobi and R. Kastenbaum (eds), *Voices and Visions of Aging: Toward a Critical Gerontology*, New York: Springer Publishing Company.

Morrow, R.A. (1991), 'Critical theory, Gramsci and cultural studies: From structuralism to poststructuralism', in P. Wexler (ed.), *Critical Theory Now*, London: Falmer Press.

Myers, J.E. (1993), 'Personal Empowerment', *Ageing International*, vol. xx, Pt. 1, 3;4; pp.6-8.

National Committee of Inquiry into Higher Education (1997), *Higher Education in the Learning Society*, London: National Committee of Inquiry into Higher Education.

Norman, A. (1987), *Aspects of Ageing: Discussion Paper*, London: Centre for Policy on Ageing.

Norton, D. (1990), *The Age of Old Age*, London: Scutari Press.

Oppenheim, C. (1993), *Poverty: The Facts*, London: Child Poverty Action Group.

Parsons, T. (1942), 'Age and sex in the social structure of the United States', *American Sociological Review*, 7, pp.614-16.

Peace, S. (ed.) (1990), *Researching Social Gerontology: Concepts, Methods and Issues*, London: Sage Publications.

Percy, K. (1990), 'Opinions, facts and hypotheses: older adults and participation in learning activities in the UK', in F. Glendenning and K. Percy (eds), *op.cit.*

Peterson, D.A. (1976), 'Educational Gerontology: the state of the art', *Educational Gerontology*, 1 (1) pp.61-73.

Peterson, D.A. (1978), 'Towards a definition of educational gerontology', in R.H. Sherron and D.B. Lumsden (eds), *op.cit.*

Peterson, D.A. (1980), 'Who are the educational gerontologists?', *Educational Gerontology*, 5(1) pp.65-77.

Peterson, D.A. (1990), 'The history of the education of the older learner', in Sherron and Lumsden (eds), *op.cit.* (3rd edition).

Peterson, D.A. (1983), *Facilitating Education for Older Learners*, San Francisco: Jossey-Bass.

Phillipson, C. (1977), *The Emergence of Retirement*, Working Papers on Sociology, No.14, Durham: University of Durham.

Phillipson, C. (1982), *Capitalism and the Construction of Old Age*, London: Macmillan.

Phillipson, C. (1985), 'Pre-retirement education in Britain and the USA', in F. Glendenning (ed.), *op.cit.*

Phillipson, C. (1988), *Reconstructing Old Age: New Agendas in Social Theory and Practice*, London: Sage Publications.

Phillipson, C. (1994), *Modernity, Postmodernity and the Sociology of Ageing: Reformulating Critical Gerontology*, Paper presented at the XII World Congress of Sociology.

Phillipson, C. and Strang, P. (1983), *the Impact of Pre-Retirement education: A Longitudinal Evaluation*, Keele: University of Keele, Department of Adult Education.

Phillipson, C. and Walker, A. (1986), *Ageing and Social Policy: A Critical Assessment*, Aldershot: Gower.

Radcliffe, D. (1984), 'The international perspectives for U3As', in E. Midwinter (ed.), *op.cit.*

Ramji, S. (1995), 'Humanizing health promotion: maximizing health', *The Older Learner: A publication of the Older Adult Education Network, American Society on Aging*, 3(4), pp.6-8.

Ramji, S. (1997), *Empowerment of Seniors in Southern Africa through Local Elderly Groups* (LEG). Paper presented to a symposium, 'Empowering senior citizens around the world through education', 1997 World Congress of Gerontology, Adelaide, Australia, August 19-34.

Rawls, J. (1971), *A Theory of Justice*, Clarendon Press, Oxford.

Rawls, J. (1996), *Political Liberalism*, Columbia University Press, New York.

Reeves, J. (1980), *The Universities of the Third Age*, Dip. Adult Education, University of London (unpublished).

Robb, B. (1967), *Sans Everything: A Case to Answer*, Edinburgh: Nelson.

Roberts, R. (1978), *The Classic Slum: Salford Life in the First Quarter of a Century*, Harmondsworth: Penguin.

Roberto, K.A., Van, A.S., and Orleans, M. (1994), 'Caregiver Empowerment Project: Developing programs within rural communities', *Activities, Adaptation and Aging*, vol 18, 2, pp.1-12.

Ross, C. (1991), 'Sports, culture and the baby boom generation in 2021', Address to *Don't Keep Your Head Down: Facing the Impact of Retirement Today and Tomorrow*, A conference sponsored by the Gerontology Research Centre, Simon Fraser University at Harbour Centre, Vancouver, BC, September 11 and 12.

Ruth, J-E. and Keynon, G. (1996), 'Biography on adult development and aging', in J.E. Birren, G.M. Kenyon, J-E. Ruth, J. Schroots and T. Svensson, T. (eds), *Aging and Biography*. New York: Springer Publishing Co. pp.1-20.

Sargant, N. (1997), *The Learning Divide: A Study of Participation in Adult Learning in the UK*, Leicester: National Institute for Adult Continuing Education.

Schaie, K.W. (1990), 'Intellectual development in adulthood', in J.E. Birren and K.W. Schaie (eds), *Handbook of the Psychology of Ageing,* 3rd edition, San Diego: Academic Press.

Schon, D. (1983), *The Reflective Practitioner: How Professionals Think in Action,* New York: Basic Books.

Schaie, K.W. and Achenbaum, W.A. (eds) (1993), *Societal Impact on Aging.* New York: Springer Publishing Company.

Schuller, T. and Bostyn, A-M. (1992), 'Learning, Education, Training and Information in the Third Age', *Carnegie Inquiry into the third Age Research Paper No. 3,* Dunfermline: Carnegie UK Trust.

Sedlak, B. (1995), 'Sharing the Leadership in Retirement', *The Older Learner,* 3(1), p.7.

Sherron, R.H. and Lumsden, D.B. (1978), *An Introduction to Educational Gerontology,*(1st edition), Washington D.C.: Hemisphere Publishing.

Slater, R. (1995), *The Psychology of Growing Old,* Buckingham: Open University Press.

Smeaton, D. and Hancock, R. (1995), *Pensioners' Expenditure,* London: Age Concern Institute of Gerontology, King's College London.

Smyth, D. (1992), 'Teachers' work and the politics of reflection', *American Educational Research Journal,* 29 (2), pp.267-300.

Stuart-Hamilton, I. (1994), *The Psychology of Ageing,* London: Jessica Kingsley Publishers.

Taylor, C. (1989), *Sources of the Self,* Cambridge: Cambridge University Press.

Tebb, S. (1995), 'An Aid to Empowerment: A caregiver well-being scale', *Health and Social Work,* vol. 20, p.2.

Thomson, D. (1983), 'Workhouse to nursing home: residential care of elderly people in England since 1840', *Ageing and Society,* 3(1), pp.43-69.

Thurz, D. (1993), 'The Possibilities of Empowerment', *Ageing International,* vol. xx, Pt. 1, pp.1-2.

Tight, M. (1998), 'Education, education, education! The vision of lifelong learning in the Kennedy, Dearing and Fryer reports', *Oxford Review of Education,* 24 (4), pp. 473-85.

Townsend, P. (1957), *The Family Life of Older People,* London: Routledge and Kegan Paul.

Townsend, P. (1962), *The Last Refuge,* London: Routledge and Kegan Paul.

Townsend, P. (1981), 'The structured dependency of the elderly: The creation of social policy in the twentieth century', *Ageing and Society,* 1(1): pp.5-28.

Townsend, P. (1986), 'Ageism and social policy', in C. Phillipson and A. Walker (eds), *op.cit.*

Tuckett, A. (1999), 'Who's Learning What?', *The Guardian,* 18 May: 13.

Tunstall, J. (1966), *Old and Alone.* London: Routledge and Kegan Paul.

Tyler, W. (1979), 'Segregated or integrated classes?', in *Adult Teaching Methods,* Leicester: National Institute for Adult Continuing Education.

Tyler, W. (1991), 'The state of educational gerontological research and philosophy in Britain', *Journal of Educational Gerontology,* 6(2) pp.70-9.

UNESCO (n.d. 1979?), *Educational Questions Concerning Education and the Elderly,* Parish: UNESCO.

Usher, R., Bryant, I. and Johnston, R. (1997), *Adult Education and the Postmodern Challenge,* London: Routledge.

Vincent, J. A, (1995), *Inequality in Old Age,* London: UCL Press.

Walker, A. (1981), 'Towards a political economy of old age', *Ageing and Society,* 1(1): 73-94.

Walker, A. (1983), 'Social policy and dependency of elderly people in Great Britain: The structure of dependent and economic status in old age', in A. Gillemard (ed.), *Old Age and the Welfare State,* Beverley Hills, CA: Sage Publications.

Walker, A. (1996), *The New Generational Contract: Intergenerational Relations, Old Age and Welfare,* London: UCL Press.

Walker, A. (1997), *Ageing Europe,* Buckingham: Open University Press.

Walker, J. (1985), 'Older people as consumers of education: the politics of participation and provision', in F. Glendenning (ed.), *op.cit.*

Walker, J. (1998), 'Mapping the learning of older adults', *Adults Learning,* 10 (2), pp.14-16.

Wallerstein, N. (1992), 'Powerlessness, empowerment, and health: Implications for Health Promotion programs', *American Journal of Health Promotion,* 6(3), pp.197-205.

Wallerstein, N. and Bernstein, E. (1988), 'Empowerment education: Freire's ideas adapted to health education', *Health Education Quarterly,* vol. 15, pp.379-394.

Ward, K. and Taylor, R. (1986), *Adult Education and the Working Class: Education for the Missing Millions,* London: Croom Helm.

Warnes, A.M. (1989), *Human Ageing and Later Life: Multidisciplinary Perspectives,* London: Edward Arnold.

Webster, R. (1997), *The European Advocacy Project,* Paper presented to a symposium, 'Empowering senior citizens around the world through education', 1997 World Congress of Gerontology, Adelaide, Australia, August 19-34.

Withnall, A. (1992), 'Towards a philosophy of educational gerontology: the unfinished deabte', *Journal of Educational Gerontology,* 7 (2), pp.16-24.

Withnall, A. and Percy, K. (1994), *Good Practice in the Education and Training of Older Adults,* Aldershot: Ashgate.

Whittaker, T. (1997), 'Rethinking elder abuse: towards an integrated theory of elder abuse', in P. Decalmer and F. Glendenning (eds), *op.cit.*

Wood, J.B., Parham, I. and Teitlman, J. (1989), 'Facing the future: interdisicplinary issues and agendas', in N.J. Osgood and A.H.L. Sontz (eds), *The Science and Practice of Gerontology*, London: Jessica Kingsley Publishers, pp.161-80.

Index

and education 21
critical thinking 71-2

demographic factor 2
Department of Education and
    Employment 4, 88
Department of Education and
    Science 2
discriminatory practices 56-7
disempowerment 64

earnings 40
education 52
  for older adults 'movement' 1, 2
  statutory provision 3
  1944 Education Act 45
  self-help 5
  and rights 2
  and emancipation 5
  vocational and non-vocational 19
  as a basic right 102
educational gerontology 10, 11, 15,
    36, 52, 55, 57, 58, 59, 80, 84,
    101
  and social gerontology 77-86
  in the USA 77
educational system 5
educational activities for older
    people 3
éducation permanante 4
empowering andragogy 67
empowerment 61-76
  and decision-making 65
  and leadership 65
equality of opportunity 50, 58
Estes, C. 17, 18, 21, 25, 63
  and the ageing enterprise 47
ethics and morality 49-59
Evans, N. 22, 23

Fennell, G. 16

Forum for the Rights of Older
    People to Education 2
Francophone countries 4
Friere, P. 18, 23, 62
functionalist paradigm 15, 16, 21,
    84

General Household Survey 7
gerogogy 23, 24
gerontological education 53, 55, 80
gerontology 25, 27
  critical 34
  education 83
  instrumental 27
Gibson, R. 5, 14, 16, 21
Glendenning, F. 2, 11, 13, 26, 27,
    43, 51, 87, 92, 93, 95
Gramsci, A. 18, 22
Groombridge, B. 5, 9, 21, 23

Harrison, R. 14
Havighurst, R.J. 19
hegemony 18, 21, 22

individual liberation 70
intergenerational value systems 54

Kennedy Report 53-4
Knowles, M. 20, 81

Laslett, P. 1, 5, 64
leadership training 66, 68
learning experience 5
Learning and Skills Council 88
Learning to succeed 88
Leonard, P. 29
liberal education 54
lifelong learning 14, 57-99, 101
lifelong education 3, 7
Lifetime learning 4
life course 28, 36, 47
Londoner, C.A. 19

Lowy, L. 9, 80, 99
Lukes, S. 58
Lumsden, D.B. 86

McEwan, E. 91, 113
McLusky, H. 10
McPherson, B.D. 85

Mary, K. 26
Minkler, M. 61, 63
Minkler, M. and Estes, C. 37
Moody, H.R. 10, 14, 27, 34, 63, 78
morally relevant criteria 54
myths 41

National Adult Learning Survey 7,
    13
National Assistance Act (1948) 44
National Health Service and
    Community Care Act (1990)
    44
National Institute for Adult
    Continuing Education 3, 5, 35,
    90

old age 61, 78
  crisis of 27
  and life course 28
  stereotype of 48
  in contemporary society 59
    older people
  and education 52
  and empowerment 16, 65
  and emancipation 34
  and identity problems 29, 32
  and life course 36
  and rights 36, 44
  and segregation 71
  and self 31
  as teachers 65
Older and Bolder project 3, 90, 91,
    102

overlapping consensus 55-6

Parsons, T. 16, 19
Peace, S. 85
pensions 40
Percy, K. 7, 24
Peterson, D.A. 9, 13, 77, 79, 84
Phillips Committee 28
Phillipson, C. 2, 15, 16, 17, 18, 25,
    27, 28, 40, 43, 45, 61, 63, 78,
    92, 94
Phillipson, C. and Strang P. 36
Poor Law 39, 44, 47
postmodern society 27, 29, 27, 31
post-work education 87, 88, 89, 97
poverty and enfeeblement 39, 40
power 66
Pre-Retirement Association 2, 96
preparation for retirement 36
political economy 25
pre-retirement education 3, 36
professional gerontology 83

quality of life 49
Radcliffe, D. 1, 8
reflective practice 23
research 65, 96
retirement 53
Roberts, R. 40
Royal Society of Arts 9
Royal Commission on Population
    28

Sargent, N. 7
Schaie, W. 43
Schon, D. 24
Schuller, T. And Bostyn, A.-M. 7,
    34, 35, 36
Sherron, R.H. and Lumsden, D.B.
    11, 77, 83, 84, 86
Simon Fraser University,
    Vancouver 62

117